TRADITION AND CHANGE

A

TRADITION AND CHANGE

Studies in Contemporary Literature

By
ARTHUR WAUGH

Essay Index Reprint Series

BOOKS FOR LIBRARIES PRESS
FREEPORT, NEW YORK

First Published 1919

Reprinted 1969

STANDARD BOOK NUMBER:
8369-1316-7

LIBRARY OF CONGRESS CATALOG CARD NUMBER:
79-93385

PRINTED IN THE UNITED STATES OF AMERICA

CONTENTS

To

Evelyn Arthur St. John Waugh

My dear Evelyn,

I do not go into the old nursery now so often as I used ; it is too full of memories to be altogether comfortable. But I found myself there last night, looking for one of the many pictures you painted there last holidays ; and, as my eye wandered round the familiar walls, I felt that the room might well serve as a sort of treasure-house of our happy home life. I remembered days when it rang with the sound of battle, and all the tea-things were broken by a flying dart. I remembered its transformation into a theatre, where Philippa made her " first appearance upon any stage " (and now she is standing before the garish blaze of real footlights). I saw it still decorated with Alec's cricket and football groups upon one wall ; and then I turned to the other, which you and Barbara have frescoed with strange Cubist pictures; and I did not forget that it had been renamed the " Studio "—your private temple of the most modern school of art. The room has changed many times since the summer when we built Underhill; but the good sound walls and timbers are still the same, and sometimes, when the house is silent in sleep, they may well whisper to one another of many cheerful hours, enshrining the same spirit as of old, although we ourselves have all grown so much older.

In memory of that room, and of all that it has seen, I should like to offer you this book, which is, in its way, only another tribute to the passage of Time, the certainty of Change, and the imperishable influence of Tradition. You are born into an era of many changes; and, if I know you at all, you will be swayed and troubled by many of them. But you are not yet so wedded to what is new that you seem likely to despise what is old. You may copy the Cubist in your living room, but an Old Master hangs above your bed. You may accept the new social order of to-morrow, but your hope is still rooted (and long may it remain so) in the old Faith that is the same yesterday, to-day, and for ever. I wish you nothing better than to change gently, like the old room where we have spent so many happy hours, reflecting the wiser fashions of the passing day, but still looking out, through sunlit casements, upon green trees, a garden of flowers, and God's blue sky above you. If that is not the happy life, I do not know where happiness is to be found.

Your loving Father,

ARTHUR WAUGH.

February 6*th*, 1919.

TRADITION AND CHANGE

HUMAN life is torn asunder by the elements of stress and change; but perhaps there is no period so poignant in its sense of solitude as that in which a man of middle-age begins to realise that he is falling out of harmony with the world around him. For everyone there strikes the hour in which, like the sudden writing on the wall, the message comes to him that his generation is over; that his tastes are weighed in the balance and found wanting; that the dreams of his youth are the common dreams of Youth no more. And the keener his sense of vitality has been in the past, the more bitter is this sudden awakening to the implacable demands of the present. He desires vehemently, it may be, to keep pace with "the great mundane movement." With every apparent sincerity he exclaims with the poet:

> Change is the pulse of life on earth;
> The artist dies, but Art lives on;
> New rhapsodies are ripe for birth
> When every rhapsodist seems gone. . . .
>
> So, to my day's extremity,
> May I, in patience infinite,
> Attend the beauty that must be,
> And, though it slay me, welcome it.

He repeats the words with a conviction of their truth; but he is only too pitiably conscious of the fact that, however much he strives to deceive himself, there is a great deal which the young men proclaim as beautiful that seems to him intolerably ugly; that many things are said nowadays which his instinctive and trained reticence would gladly have left unsaid; that Youth has got the bit between its teeth; and that, even if he would, he is helpless to restrain its headlong course.

And then, perhaps, he looks back, and recalls his own young days: the puzzled brow of a father who found him—yes, even him—a disturbing rebel: the protests to which he had no leisure to attend: the voluble companions, now scattered if not for ever silent, who have long since been relegated to the limbo of an outworn fashion. How quickly the years have gone, since he himself seemed to stand on the threshold of a new heaven and a new earth! How suddenly the raïnbow faded: how soon the bright gold grew dim! Tradition and Change: it is the perpetual conflict of the ages. Who can hope to retain the heart of youth, when once the foot is weary and the eye grown dim? And who can discriminate justly between the ideals by which he was fostered and fed, and those that his children assure him are the only perfect password to wisdom and to truth?

The reader will not have turned over many pages of these collected essays before he appreciates that they are the expression of a type of mind trained to Victorian standards, tortured—it may be—by the spiritual doubts and hopes which seemed so vital to the age of Darwin, and presided over, in poetry and prose, by the strong and confident personalities of Tennyson and

Browning, of Thackeray, Dickens, and all the great Victorian host.

The spirit of that time was in many essential points in direct variance with the spirit of the present hour. Its very watchword was Caution. The middle-class, that rose into significance after the passing of the Reform Bill, was a class of firm and sincere ambition, conservative at heart, yet already stretching out its hands towards a wider emancipation. It distrusted passion, deprecated haste, was afraid of rebellion. It loved its country blindly, was somewhat insular in outlook, and believed in that steady, premeditated kind of reform, which made its ground good before it ventured to advance. Its faith took the easy-going form of Broad Churchmanship, and was much concerned to reconcile the discoveries of science with the traditions of belief. It was terribly afraid of democracy, which it recognised at work all around it, and which it regarded as the harbinger of anarchy in thought and life ; its creed was founded on a complete trust in the necessity of Law and Order, as much in Art as in Morals. And, although we have, most of us, broken free from some or other of these spiritual captivities, we are all the creatures of our birth and breeding, and such a survey as is attempted in these pages must necessarily bear about it the marks of its heredity and its training. Its limitations will be self-evident ; but at any rate, it is sincere. And those who find it least open to new impressions will, perhaps, be generous enough to believe that it also represents an honest effort to recognise the value of as much of the new spirit as seems reasonably consonant with old standards: the effort of one who would gladly be young again, if he could; and who only raises his voice in protest, and that with hesitation, when fresh experiments appear too dangerously opposed to the permanent traditions of the art we all seek to serve, however humbly, in our quickly-transient hour.

Tradition, after all, has its due; it is vindicated upon every page of the British treasury of poetry and prose. The manner of the great masters is irresistible: it never falls out of fashion; its colours never fade; even the young men would catch its echoes, if they knew how. But, just as in the world of politics and society we seem for the moment to be trembling upon the verge of anarchy, so in contemporary literature there is, surely, a pervading peril lest, in our persistent search after novelty, we lose touch with the one and only safe antiseptic of all Art, the immortal and imperishable sense of Form.

The form, the form alone is eloquent.

Whatever else is open to question, that at least is sure. Without Form there can be no true literature, without Beauty the art of the poet languishes and falls into dust. It is true, no doubt, that the blind pursuit of beauty has in the past led many into the morass of insipidity: it is even truer that grace without strength withers in a sort of effeminate pose. Twenty or thirty years ago Poetry was indeed threatened with the inevitable penalty of over-refinement, and the fiction of the day was drowned out with intolerable sentimentality. No one, to be sure, could bring any such accusation, with justice, against the representative literature of the present time. The risk has now swung to the other pole. The most insidious perils of to-day are the perils of violence and crudity, of a passion for originality at any cost, of eccentricity in form and of vulgarity in matter. Surely it will never be without profit to remember that eccentricity has invariably headed towards its own downfall, and that the vulgarity of one age becomes the universal detestation of the next.

The essays here collected will, it is hoped, be found to touch upon many different manifestations of the writer's art, and to bear witness to an insatiable desire to establish terms of sympathy with literary temperaments of widely divergent scope. But through them all there will probably be traced a single prevailing concept —the estimate of literature which Oxford was accustomed to instil into her sons as the very birthright of her citizenship—that all sound literary expression must maintain its loyalty to the high traditions of the past, and that the very essences of its being are beauty of imagination and dignity of utterance. The point of view must inevitably change, as social horizons widen, and the claims of individuality assert themselves. But even the rebel himself is most persuasive when he captures the voice of authority: the one form of speech intolerable to the true orator is the incorrigible garrulity of the tavern Gargantuan. The enormously increased influence of journalism has, no doubt, much to answer for. Books and their writers are frequently written about nowadays in a loosely-familiar and ogling fashion that used to be confined to the records of society favourites and the much-photographed heroines of the footlights. Personality of this kind is bound to vulgarise art ; publicity breeds an irresistible itch for vulgar display. But the great writers of the past were generally content with the praise of their peers : their sense of self-respect was sufficient recompense. The change that defies the tradition of restraint is a change in the fatal direction of commercialism and decay.

But, even so, the critic must be careful of his steps, for he can scarcely hope to escape from the nets which his inherited prejudices and predilections have woven about his feet. And the first obligation of a book like the present is to make what possible peace it may with its readers, deprecating with the most complete sincerity any claim to reflect more than a limited outlook upon life and letters, and acknowledging the enormous difficulty of holding fast to a true tradition in the midst of an overwhelming whirlpool of change. We can see very little of the truth, every one of us : we are all let and hindered by an inextricable web of circumstance. The most we can do is to be loyal to the faith in which we were bred, hoping that the faith that has helped us may not be altogether illusion, and that it may even be of some help to others much younger, and much wiser (no doubt) than ourselves. At any rate, it has been our own faith, the tradition that has carried us through the changes of this distractingly changeful life. We cherish it for its long association ; and we hand it on, such as it is, to the judgment of that younger generation which is waiting to take our place, as soon as we can decently make ready to be gone.

STUDIES IN POETRY

THE NEW POETRY

1. *Georgian Poetry* 1911-12. The Poetry Bookshop, 1912.
2. *Georgian Poetry* 1913-15. The Poetry Bookshop, 1915.
3. *The Catholic Anthology* 1914-15. Elkin Mathews, 1915.

THE difficulty which has always beset criticism in its attempts to arrive at a satisfactory definition of the word Poetry is by no means confined to the elusive nature of the art itself. For not only is the art of Poetry so sensitive and subtle as to escape again and again from the process of analysis, but the very standards by which it is controlled are continually changing, and the artist's own conception of his business is in a state of perpetual transition. Religion, philosophy, imagination, fancy, rebellion, and reaction—these, and many other elements in human thought, have left their impress upon the poetic tradition; and the function of criticism, as each new generation breaks with some established canon, has been more and more to hold to what is best in tradition, to test new movements in the light of that best, and yet to keep an open mind towards innovations, and to welcome any change, however revolutionary, that is calculated to enlarge the field of poetic vision and activity. This last function is the hardest of all the tasks that criticism is called upon to undertake; but the more intelligently the critic embraces it, the better will he fulfil his responsibilities. The history of literature has proved with weary iteration that the worst and most retarding fault that criticism can commit is the tendency to doubt every new movement, and to challenge and defy methods whose novelty may indeed be disconcerting, and yet may contain the germ of artistic emancipation and enlightenment.

It behoves the critic, therefore, to walk warily among new movements, without losing touch with the permanent laws of his craft; and, to guide him amid all minor differences of period and taste, there will be found certain main conceptions of the poetic art, which have stood fast in the face of change and revolution. Preeminent among these, the very charter of Poetry itself, is the conception that poetry consists in the imputation of universality to the individual idea and impulse; and conversely in the interpretation of the individual impulse in the light of universal truth. The personal quality of the emotion or impulse expressed has been always regarded as essential, because it is only through personality that the artist can make his appeal. But the individual personality acquires acceptance precisely as it relates itself to the universal heart of the world. When we read a poem, or a passage in a poem, and exclaim instinctively: "That is true. I never thought it before, but now it is said, I recognise it as true, and as so well said that it is never likely to be said better": when, in short, we find ourselves face to face with an eternal idea expressed in flawless language, we acknowledge instinctively that we are in the presence of poetry of the essential, classic order, against which time and the ebbing tide of taste are powerless. But there must be this complete fusion of thought with expression. The qualities of form, beauty, and music, which tradition has accepted as inseparable from poetry, remain inseparable from it to-day. Without the universal, living idea, embodying itself in personal experience, you may have agreeable, charming verse, but you cannot have poetry. And, with equal emphasis, unless the idea is clothed in language that fits it, embodies it, and gives it poetic currency, you may have rhetoric and eloquence, but you will not and cannot have poetry. For poetry so indissolubly blends the universal and the personal that idea, image, expression, and symbol are indistinguishable from one another in the perfected harmony of their union.

These considerations (trite enough, perhaps, in themselves) would appear to be worth recalling at the present time, since there is evidently some danger of their being forgotten in the indefatigable search for novelty and sensation which, after vexing the field of the English novel with varying fortunes, has recently attacked the poet's art as well. We have been passing through a period of intellectual transition and readjustment. The stirring and revolutionary movements which convulsed the Victorian era have exhausted themselves; the world of ideas has grown stagnant; and the art of poetry has made but little recognisable advance for a period of something like twenty years. And now we are suddenly confronted by a new movement, on whose behalf the claim is made that " English poetry is once again putting on a new strength and beauty," so that " we are at the beginning of another Georgian period which may take rank in due time with the several great poetic ages of the past." These are proud words ; and one of the most conspicuous revolutionists of the new school has elsewhere defined the movement with which he is identified in no uncertain terms. " Our aim," he says, " is natural speech, the language as spoken. We desire the words of poetry to follow the natural order. We would write nothing that we might not say actually in life—under emotion." It is, perhaps, not surprising to learn, as we do in the same context, that the herald of this new standard of poetry has " degrees of antipathy and even contempt for Milton and Victorianism and the softness of the nineties ; "* and, though it is improbable that his disgust with what he describes as " the Miltonian quagmire " would be endorsed by many of the other champions of Georgian Poetry, it is at least certain that the atmosphere of all the three volumes cited at the head of this article is an atmosphere of empirical rebellion. Since, moreover, this atmosphere of rebellion is introduced with a confidence quite gloriously cocksure, it may not be without value to consider the claims of these young innovators, and to estimate the effect which their influence seems likely to exercise upon English poetry in the immediate future. It is evident that such influence is by no means negligible, for the first anthology of Georgian

* "The Poems of Lionel Johnson." With an Introduction by Ezra Pound. Elkin Mathews.

Poetry is already in a twelfth impression, and many of the names that decorate it are among the most enthusiastically acclaimed of the younger generation. But, before we consider their performance in detail, a few reflections upon the art which they practise may help us to appreciate the precise standard of poetry to which their workmanship and spiritual outlook conform.

Poetry, it will be generally conceded, even by the most enterprising claimant for plain speaking in common speech, must work in one or other, or in all combined, of three different media—ideas, emotions, and moods. When poetry was defined as "a criticism of life," the framer of the definition had in mind chiefly the poetry of ideas; when it is described as "emotion remembered in tranquillity," the description is directed chiefly to emotional poetry; and when we are told, as we often are nowadays, that the sincere reproduction of a moment's spiritual experience is the proper concern of the poetic art, this third and final definition applies almost exclusively to the poetry which seeks to reproduce the writer's passing mood without considering its permanent truth or value. The highest order of poetry will be found, under analysis, to combine elements from each of these three classes; for the emotion, without which poetry is barren, contains in itself an indirect reference to the mood in which it is evoked, while the poet proceeds from the registration of the emotion to test it by the standard of the universal idea. But it must never be forgotten that the idea is the germ of the poem; that the truth and universality of the idea is the test of the poem's quality;

and that, as poetry recedes from the region of ideas into that of emotions, and sinks still further from emotions into moods, it retires more and more from that high vantage ground from whose summit the classic poetry of the ages overlooks the manifold activity of the world. From the idea to the emotion, and from the emotion to the mood, is a downward path, separating poetry from its high, universal significance, and bringing it step by step nearer to a condition of anarchy, in which every individual's claim is paramount, where Art can represent nothing permanent since nothing permanent or stable exists within its survey to be represented.

Now a careful examination of these two volumes of Georgian poetry seems to suggest that during the last ten years or so English poetry has been approaching a condition of poetic liberty and licence which threatens, not only to submerge old standards altogether, but, if persevered in to its logical limits, to hand over the sensitive art of verse to a general process of literary democratisation. For some time before this movement took shape, the powers of reaction had been at work upon English poetry. The Pre-Raphaelite movement, for example, was in itself a reaction. It found the soulful earnestness of the Victorians quietly sinking into a sort of dogmatic philosophy. Science, religion, doubt, and faith had apparently taken the Muses' Hill by storm ; and a way of escape was sought into the dreams of the past, by reviving ideals and standards of a simpler and a more artistically-minded world. The step from such a mood to one of general discontent with all surviving traditions was but a short one ; and the next step after that is inevitably the complete abandonment of tradition and standard alike. " We write nothing that we might not speak," proclaims the new rebellion in effect : " we draw the thing as we see it for the God of things as they are. Every aspect of life shall be the subject of our art, and what we see we will describe in the language which we use every day. The result shall be the New Poetry, the vital expression of a new race."

To such a manifesto, even before its artistic achievements come to be examined, there is one preliminary reply. It is indeed true that the artificer may put whatever he sees into his melting-pot, but it by no means follows that he will get a work of art out of his mould. It may be arguable that the poet should shovel the language of the mining-camp into his lyric, but it is more than doubtful whether poetry will emerge. Force may emerge, vigour may emerge, an impressive and vital kind of rhetoric may take form from the composition ; but poetry is something more than these. Poetry must possess beauty ; beauty is the essence of its being ; and it has never been the general experience that the language of the common crowd possesses either beauty or authority. When poetry proposes to confine itself to the commercial counters of speech, the first thing we should expect would be a failure in dignity and charm. When it sets itself to break loose from the traditions of structure and harmony, the next inevitable consequence would be the wastage of form and melody. And emphatically enough, the very first impression with which the reader of these volumes of Georgian poetry is assailed is an impression of a fitful lack of dignity, and a recurrent tendency to neglect the claims of form and structure, which continually distract the reader's attention from his author's meaning, by thrusting into the foreground a sense of the unrestrained and even violent fashion in which that meaning is striving to get itself expressed. That the form of expression has crude energy, rising at intervals into power, we do not dispute ; but it is emphatically the sort of energy that has not hitherto been associated with the methods and aims of poetry.

The blank verse of Mr. Wilfrid Wilson Gibson, for example, has evidently thrown aside in weariness the golden foot-rule of the Augustans :

For sure enough the camel's old evil incarnate ! . . .
The only moments I've lived my life to the full
And that live again in remembrance unfaded are those
When I've seen life compact in some perfect body. . . .

It would be amusing to hear Dr. Johnson's comments upon this turbulent kind of prosody. Such liberties with his favourite ten-syllabled line might well " perturbate his paradisal state," torturing it into one of fuliginous thunderstorm. But Mr. Lascelles Abercrombie's blank verse is yet more rough and unmelodious :

Anger was smarting in my eyes like grit.
O the fine earth and fine all for nothing !
Mazed I walkt, seeing and smelling and hearing :
The meadowlands all shining fearfully gold,—

> Cruel as fire the sight of them toucht my mind ;
> Breathing was all a honeytaste of clover
> And beanflowers. I would have rather had it
> Carrion, or the stink of smouldering brimstone.

Now, it is evident that the writer who sets down such unmetrical lines as these is writing in deliberate defiance of metrical tradition. No man, possessed by the impulse to express himself in verse, was ever the victim of so bad an ear as to believe that

> O the fine earth and fine all for nothing !

is a reasonable line of blank-verse as it was understood by the classicists. But Mr. Abercrombie would very properly reply that he is not writing for the classicists at all, but for the young bloods of the twentieth century, and that he chooses to write like this for the sake of avoiding monotony and of achieving sudden and vigorous effect. Well, as a matter of fact, is the effect really heightened by this kind of incoherent violence ? Is it not rather true that the description in the first passage quoted above is so confused and involved that the lines must be read twice before they take hold upon the imagination, and that even then the final impression left by them is one of an imperfect and unfinished draft ? Vehemence without corresponding effect is nothing worth ; it resembles the volubility of an unpractised orator, and the taint of undisciplined experiment too frequently affects and mars Mr. Abercrombie's workmanship. His " Sale of St. Thomas " has a fine imaginative idea at the heart of it ; it is, in fact, one of the few poems in the collection which deal with an idea of permanent significance and original force. St. Thomas is conceived as torn asunder between a divine impulse to carry on the work of his Master and a restraining prudence, which perpetually retards his mission by suggesting the risks and perils of the enterprise. Finally the Master reappears and sells St. Thomas into bondage. For fear, He says, is a venial failing,

But prudence, prudence is the deadly sin,
And one that groweth deep into a life
With hardening roots that clutch about the breast.
For this refuses faith in the unknown powers
Within man's nature ; shrewdly bringeth all
Their inspiration of strange eagerness
To a judgment bought by safe experience ;
Narrows desire into the scope of thought.

Here is a fine animating theme for poetry, and one well suited to a muse bent upon new adventure ; but throughout the poem, as even more noticeably in his breathless, exclamatory drama " The End of the World," the poet appears to have hurled himself into the effort of creation before properly digesting his material, and to be content to accept as finished work what ought to have been recognised as the first rough notes, or " trial balance " of his composition. He is so eager to be trying conclusions with the new idea that he exhausts himself in a single flight, and never advances beyond the initial phases of the experiment.

This restlessness seems to be growing upon the poet, for his earlier work showed imagination much more satisfactorily at one with its material. His *vers libre*, which is now often crude and shapeless, had at first a genuine justification, in its courageous attempt to break free once and for all from the mild fluidity of the Tennysonian euphuists. He introduced a degree of elasticity and variety into the metre which was stimulating to the ear, while the eye was continually fed by rich and clustered imagery :

The world's a flame of the unquenching fire,
An upward-rapturing unhindered flame,
Singing a golden praise that it can be,
One of the joys of God the eternal fire.
But than this soaring nature, this green flame,
Largely exulting, not knowing how to cringe,
God's joy, there are things even sacreder,
Words : they are messengers from out God's heart,
Intimate with him ; through his deed they go,
This passion of him called the world, approving
All of fierce gladness in it, bidding leap
To a yet higher rapture ere it sink.

And again, in the lyric metre of the choruses in "Peregrinus" there was a haunting beauty, which appears too rarely in his later work :

Little flames, merry flames, modest low chucklings,
This is but maidenly pretence of shyness ;
Little flames, happy flames, what are these secrets
You so modestly whisper one another ?
Do we not know your golden desires,
And the brave way you tower into lust
Mightily shameless ?
Why do you inly skulk among the timber ?
Stand up, yellow flames, take the joy given you ;
Resins and spunkwood, faggots and turpentine,
A deal of spices, a great cost of benzoin,
Everything proper for your riot, O flames.

It is a great pity that a sort of impulsive impatience should mar such genuine ability, but it is difficult to resist the impression that Mr. Abercrombie is in danger of accepting everything that occurs spasmodically to his fancy as the finished product of a meditative art.

Something of the same haste and impatient negligence of technique disfigures the work of Mr. Walter De la Mare, who aims at a simpler form of fantasy than Mr. Abercrombie, only again and again to spoil a dainty fancy by wayward affectations and clumsy inversions :

Three jolly Farmers
Once bet a pound
Each dance the others would
Off the ground.
Out of their coats
They slipped right soon,
And neat and nicesome
Put each his shoon.

An onomatopoetic measure like this, chosen to reproduce the spirit of the dance, is absolutely ruined by such tortured phrases as weigh down the third, seventh, and eighth lines of this opening, and the same fault crops up all through the piece. And in " Melmillo " a gossamer imagination is marred by similar clumsiness of touch :

Three and thirty birds there stood
In an elder in a wood ;
Called Melmillo—flew off three,
Leaving thirty in the tree ;
Called Melmillo—nine now gone,
And the boughs held twenty-one ;

Called Melmillo—and eighteen
Left but three to nod and preen ;
Called Melmillo—three—two—one—
Now of birds were feathers none.

Here again the awkwardness of inversion, and the consequent suggestion of artificiality, go a long way to dispel the dainty and sincere simplicity of the picture.

But the champion of the new impressionism in poetry may reasonably rejoin that the very object, to which these young writers are bending their energies, is nothing less than emancipation from the metrical trammels of the past ; that what they particularly desire is freedom of method allied to freedom of thought ; and that their workmanship can only be judged in connexion with the ideas which it embodies. This is true enough ; all artistic technique must be largely controlled by the subject it pourtrays. We do not expect Caliban to discuss Setebos in the sublime language of the Deity musing upon the perfected beauty of Eden. But dramatic propriety is one thing, and lyrical poetry is quite another. The question is, whether lyric verse can possibly " take rank with the several great poetic ages of the past," unless thought and expression combine to produce a thing of beauty, recognisable as beautiful by any sensitive taste, and containing at the heart's core that inevitable quality of the universal which will be found to distinguish all the poetry that endures. There are certain poems in the collection to which it is possible to ascribe without hesitation this high and inalienable privilege, and it is no slight vindication of the standards of the past that they are all poems conceived and executed in the soundest tradition of fine workmanship.

Let us take, for instance, Mr. Sturge Moore's "Sicilian Idyll," which is not only the most striking poem in the earlier volume, but may be said to present, in an allegory, the complete philosophy of the poetic movement which it adorns. An aged couple in a Sicilian village are immersed in the mild atmosphere of repose and acquiescence which middle-age brings to those who have escaped from the disturbing passions of youth. Damon with his wine-bowl and his gossip, and Cydilla with her ball of worsted and nimble fingers, are content enough in their back-water of life. Only one anxiety troubles them. Their son Delphis has broken loose from their uneventful home, and gone out into the world in a mist of rebellion and adventure, to warm both hands before the fire of life. What has befallen him by the way? The shadow of that anxiety is always over the old people. One day Damon meets his son again. He has become tutor to a young lad, and his imagination is aflame with the delight of moulding an impressionable soul to his own pattern. The very ecstasy of creation inspires him; and then suddenly another man crosses his path, a creature of low instincts and animal impulses, who inflames the boy's mind with unclean fancies, and seems likely in a moment to ruin the work of Delphis's long-cherished ambition. Then Delphis in his turn has to learn the lesson of the world's progress. Youth will not stay for the word of experience; the call of the wild tempts every new generation to its disaster. So Delphis, enraged with civilisation, takes the solitary way:

A vagabond I shall be as the moon is.
The sun, the waves, the winds, all birds, all beasts
Are ever on the move, and take what comes;
They are not parasites like plants and men
Rooted in that which fed them yesterday.

. . . . . .

Free minds must bargain with each greedy moment
And seize the most that lies to hand at once.
Ye are too old to understand my words;
I yet have youth enough, and can escape
From that which sucks each individual man
Into the common dream.

What is this but the perfect apologia for the wandering life of an art which makes no compromise with tradition, an apologia expressed in language of great force, sincerity, and persuasiveness?

But the apologia is double-edged. For the wanderer goes his way, drifting without purpose upon a rudderless course, while the little citadel of civilisation stands firm, because man is a social being, and it is through the self-sacrifice of the individual that the life of each generation is made easier than the last. And so, after Delphis has raved himself out of sight, the last word is with the old parents, as they gather up the worsted and the knitting, and trot off in search of their son's pupil "to offer their poor service in his stead."

We must be doing something, for I feel
We both shall drown our hearts with time to spare.

Man cannot live for himself alone ; his past and present must control the laws for his future. Nor can the artist separate himself from the traditions of his art, and start afresh upon a new programme with each new generation. The continuity of life and of art is alike unbroken ; there is nothing really new nor isolated under the sun.

But Mr. Sturge Moore has disappeared from the later volume of Georgian Poetry, whether because, as the editor says of absent contributors, he has " published nothing which comes within its scope," or because he " belongs in fact to an earlier poetic generation, and his inclusion must be allowed to have been an anachronism," we are not told. In any case the absence of his restrained and eloquent verse is a distinct loss to the later collection ; and it is a further, and a very real misfortune to the movement as a whole, that two of its most gifted and promising leaders have been swept away prematurely by the untimely stroke of death. In James Elroy Flecker and Rupert Brooke we gladly recognise two other poets of indisputable and glowing promise, whose influence upon their contemporaries might possibly have had the most salutary and formative results. Without them much that is left of the movement fades into a feverish confusion of experiment ; but one of these two possessed intuitively, and the other was on the point of acquiring by experience, just that quality of artistic self-control which would save them from the excesses with which they were surrounded, and leaven the modern movement as a whole with a powerful leaven of beauty and spirituality. Flecker, indeed, had little to connect him with rebellious modernity. He indulged in no half-fledged experiments, and made no attempt to shock his readers' susceptibilities. His passion was chiefly for the old—old ships, old buildings, old legends, and old loyalties ; and he sang their praise in haunting melodies which recalled the immemorial music of the old, unchangeable sea :

Evening on the olden, the golden sea of Wales,
When the first star shivers and the last wave pales :
O evening dreams !
  There's a house that Britons walked in, long ago,
  Where now the springs of ocean fall and flow,
And the dead robed in red and sea-lilies overhead
  Sway when the long winds blow.

Sleep not, my country ; though night is here, afar
Your children of the morning are clamorous for war:
Fire in the night, O dreams !
  Though she send you as she sent you, long ago,
  South to desert, east to ocean, west to snow,
West of these out to seas colder than the Hebrides
  I must go
Where the fleet of stars is anchored, and the young
  Star-captains glow.

Such melody and such imagery as this are in the true succession ; they owe nothing to any passing fashion. But Rupert Brooke was essentially in the heart of the new movement ; and his earlier work was not immune from its shortcomings both of taste and of faulty selection. He was obsessed by the modern melancholy. Fired by that love of English life and English scenery which is the hall-mark of the public school and University man, bubbling over with delight in life and love and sweet companionship, he could nevertheless rarely escape, even for an hour, from the depressing conviction of the transient quality of all beauty and all human enjoyment, even indeed of love itself.

> Magnificently unprepared
> For the long littleness of life,

he had scarcely raised its goblet to his lips, before he saw the wine turn to poison in the cup. Bright eyes, gold hair, red lips—all would be dust in a few years, blown upon the wind in solitary, loveless pilgrimage.

> And every mote, on earth or air,
>   Will speed and gleam, down later days,
> And like a secret pilgrim fare
>   By eager and invisible ways,
>
> Nor ever rest, nor ever lie,
>   Till, beyond thinking, out of view,
> One mote of all the dust that's I
>   Shall meet one atom that was you.

And then, perhaps, would be granted to the dead passion its one faint hope of immortality, that the flame of reunited love should strike into the heart of some pair of living lovers, rapt out of themselves into an unfamiliar ecstasy:

> And they will know—poor fools, they'll know!—
>   One moment, what it is to love.

The dread of the loss of individuality burned into the soul of this eager individualist, until the horror of Nirvana almost consumed his power of expression.

Oh, Heaven's Heaven !—but we'll be missing
The palms, and sunlight, and the south ;
And there's an end, I think, of kissing
When our mouths are one with Mouth. . . .

That last line, with its taint of inherent ugliness, an ugliness which becomes almost vulgar, is unfortunately characteristic of the worst side of Rupert Brooke, the itch to say a thing in such an arresting fashion as to shock the literary purist into attention even against his will. There are too many such blots upon his poetry.

Here, where love's stuff is body, arm and side
  Are stabbing-sweet 'gainst chair and lamp and wall.
In every touch more intimate meanings hide ;
  And flaming brains are the white heart of all.

This is not poetry at all ; once more we are confronted with the failure of a vehemence that loses itself in words. So too in the interminable list of material comforts which he loved (and Brooke never quite knew when to stop, when his imagination had started upon a mental catalogue), he exhausts and irritates the fancy with the suggestion of a cloistered, almost an epicurean, self-consciousness. Individualism indeed ran riot in his temperament ; but, when the call came to make the supreme sacrifice, he learnt in a sudden flash of revelation, what so many of his comrades had learnt by degrees upon the hard stones of experience, that individuality is only given to man in order that he may devote it to the service of his generation.

Now, God be thanked Who has matched us with His hour,
And caught our youth, and wakened us from sleeping,
With hand made sure, clear eye, and sharpened power,
To turn, as swimmers into cleanness leaping,
Glad from a world grown old and cold and weary,
Leave the sick hearts that honour could not move,
And half-men, and their dirty songs and dreary,
And all the little emptiness of love !
Oh ! we, who have known shame, we have found release there,
Where there's no ill, no grief, but sleep has mending,
Naught broken save this body, lost but breath ;
Nothing to shake the laughing heart's long peace there
But only agony, and that has ending ;
And the worst friend and enemy is but Death.

So invigorating, and so transcendently sincere, is this return of the poet upon the self-centred dreams of youth, with their vain regrets for the passage of beauty, that we may be excused for believing that, had Rupert Brooke survived the war, its cleansing fire would have lighted him to achievements both in life and poetry far greater than had yet been dreamed of by a philosophy so disillusioned and so disintegrate. *Dis aliter visum :* and now this bright young harbinger of beaconing possibilities sleeps by the Ægean Sea :

A dust whom England bore, shaped, made aware,
Gave, once, her flowers to love, her ways to roam,
A body of England's, breathing English air,
Washed by the rivers, blest by suns of home.

And in his grave rest, beyond doubt, the highest expectations of the poetic movement which he seemed destined, in the very hour of his death, to turn into richer and more profitable channels.

The gulf which separates these three poets from the larger body of the New Poetry may, perhaps, be bridged by Mr. John Drinkwater, who in a well-conceived and finely-written idyll gives expression to yet one more allegory of the artistic life. " The Carver in Stone " indeed is easily referable to the sister art of poetry. It tells of a sculptor, patient and idealistic, who was engaged, with a host of his fellow-workmen, to decorate the frieze of a great temple. They set to work to embody the forms of local deities, tiger, owl, bull, leopard, ram, camel, lizard, and the rest, and carved them, as the crowd preferred to find them, without life or vital meaning. The solitary artist, on the other hand, threw all his energies into the sculpture of an eagle, that spread

> Wide pinions on a cloudless ground of heaven,
> Glad with the heart's high courage of that dawn
> Moving upon the ploughlands newly sown,
> Dead stone the rest. He looked, and knew it so.

The crowd, however, looked with other eyes. The king and his counsellors flocked to inspect the work, and praised the lean, dull animals of the field. Only one critic noticed the eagle at all, and he would have preferred a swan. So the lonely artist left popularity to the others, and begged to be allowed to decorate the panels in the clerestory, unseen because no one would ever trouble to climb the winding stair. There he carved a great, squatting toad, the emblem of the crowd's " emphatic warrant," and surrounded it with the other types of the people's gods, wonderfully interpreted now in the light of their own ugliness—cruelty, fear, and servile toil. The temple was finished, and nobody climbed the stair to see his panels between the high windows, But he looked in solitude and contentment

Again upon his work, and knew it good,
Smiled on his toad, passed down the stair unseen,
And sang across the teeming meadows home.

It would not be just to carry the comparison too far ; for the fault of the New Poetry is certainly not that it lacks life, like the heavy images of the people's gods in the poem, but rather, and principally, that it lacks beauty and spirituality. Life it has in abundance, the fierce, feverish life of a mind that has not yet established its relations with its environment, and is perpetually launching excursions into new territory, without consolidating the ground that it has won. It is the life, in fact, of experiments and moods ; and the poetry in which it issues is precisely that poetry of the mood and of the emotion, which we have already defined as lacking the sound foundations and universal significance of the poetry of ideas. The general atmosphere is that of a world in which there is no prevailing current of ideas, no pervading intellectual stimulus, and from which the natural refuge is found in the exaggeration of trivial incidents into some sort of symbolic relation with big movements, and in the acceptance of individual whims and wayward fancies in the place of firm philosophic ideals.

Symbolism plays an inevitable part in such a movement; and the readiness with which symbolism runs to seed always renders it a dangerous ally of poetry. For when it gets out of hand, it is apt to trail off into a sort of entanglement of its own elaboration, growing by self-indulgence. The prolixity of the author's fancy dulls the edge of the animating idea; and this is the very foible in which the imagery of the New Poetry loses itself again and again. It gets hold of a half-developed idea, and elaborates it out of all proportion and perspective. "The Hare," by Mr. Wilfrid Gibson, a fine poem in many respects, nevertheless labours under this disadvantage. In the hunted eyes of the hare the rustic sportsman realises something of the shy apprehension of womanhood, a shyness which maternity and its consolations alone have the power to dispel. The image and the idea are true, but the poet proceeds to decorate them with all the circumstance of venery—first the pursuit of the hare, then the pursuit of the woman, and then the two pursuits merged symbolically into one; until the whole thing is so overclouded by half-realised metaphor that the main idea fades out of sight.

This fault strikes one the more strangely in Mr. Gibson's work, since his particular strength lies at the other extreme of quality. Swift vividness of impression is the essence of his art, and none among the younger writers has a surer gift for seizing upon the elements of a scene or an incident and presenting them arrestingly to the imagination. The hard, eager little poems, which he has devoted to events and impressions of the present war, furnish characteristic illustrations of his talent in this respect ; and it is curious to find, as occasionally happens in his longer flights, that his touch is capable of faltering into indecision. But, when the artist breaks free of restraining standards, it is no uncommon experience that he should lose a sense of selection also. The very vividness of his insight tempts him to multiply impressions, until they overcrowd the picture and obliterate its purpose. This is one of the most insidious dangers of realism ; and there are occasions when an even more perilous boundary gets crossed, in the poet's effort to be original and arresting at any cost.

The two pieces by Mr. D. H. Lawrence, which bear the names " The Snapdragon " and " Love and Cruelty," might well serve as cautionary examples of realism running riot in verse. Both deal with the sudden submergence of judgment and self-restraint in the clutch of gross physical passion, and both use symbols from the natural world to illustrate a degree of self-abandonment which is so invertebrate as to be practically abnormal. The sinister power of the impression is not to be denied ; but it bears no sort of affinity to poetry. It is in both cases an experiment in perverted symbolism, casting a sombre shadow upon the wholesome impulses of passion and of natural sexual attraction.

Realism, however, is no rarity among the younger poets ; and the lack of restraint which stimulates their frequent and irrelevant prolixity inspires them no less in the choice of subjects and of methods so coarse as inevitably to repel the clear, bright atmosphere of poetry altogether. Mr. John Masefield, no doubt, has done something to set the fashion, although he is only inadequately represented in these pages. But Mr. Masefield's moral narratives in verse have a powerful sense of virility behind them ; and two of them, " The Everlasting Mercy," and " The Widow in the Bye Street," whatever may be thought of their violence of taste and diction, are at any rate highly impressive homilies in metre, filled to the brim with a glowing passion for morality. Mr. Masefield, moreover, is full of the true stuff of poetry, and, when he is once at work by the countryside or on his even more familiar ocean, the splendour and variety of his imagery are impeccable. His realism also is invariably in the dramatic vein. If he is coarse, he takes his colour from the theme ; directly the theme rises in the spiritual scale, the poet's inspiration rises with it to heights that not infrequently border on sublimity. The same is true of Mr. Ralph Hodgson, who completely justifies the rather sombre realism of " The Bull " by the intense pathos and sincerity of its human allegory. Strength of this sort, even if it broadens down into crudity, is in direct harmony with its subject ; the dramatic situation requires it, and its final effect appears artistically inevitable.

The realism of Mr. Lawrence and of Mr. William Davies is of an entirely different order. Here, as in certain isolated passages in Rupert

Brooke's work, individualism bursts its bounds, and elevates a merely animal instinct into that higher region of ideas to which, of course, animal instinct has always been recognised as a congenital foe. And the result, as in " The Bird of Paradise," is sheer ugliness, an ugliness which does grave injustice to the true spirit of beauty which fills Mr. Davies's pastoral poems with sunshine and the scent of flowers in a spring breeze. It is strange, at first sight, that such aberrations of taste should exist side by side with so much natural beauty ; but they are evidently a common defect of the New Poetry, and would appear to have their root in the defiance, and consequent loss, of authority which attends all efforts to democratise society and art.

This failing is painfully evident in one of the finest and most impressive poems in either volume, the noble " King Lear's Wife " of Mr. Gordon Bottomley. Here, in a strongly-knit, vigorous, dramatic fragment, we are given a sort of prelude to Shakespeare's tragedy, and that a prelude which serves very reasonably to explain the inhuman treatment meted out to their father by Goneril and Regan at a later stage of his history. The Lear of this fragment is still a man in his prime, lusty and lustful, with a sickly dying wife who has long since ceased to satisfy his uxorious demands. Goneril is just emerging into womanhood—a huntress maid ; Cordelia is a prattling nursery child ; Regan hangs about the kitchen for scraps. Upon Goneril falls the horror of revelation, for, as her mother lies dying in the great bed, she sees her father toying in the shadow with her mother's maid, who is already destined by the doting Lear to be the moribund wife's successor, while all the time the wanton is carrying on an intrigue with a younger man in the King's retinue. The honour of the house is in Goneril's hand, and she stabs her father's paramour to death, returning with the blood upon her hands, to point the moral of a woman's intuition :

I do not understand how men can govern,
Use craft and exercise the duty of cunning,
Anticipate treason, treachery meet with treachery,
And yet believe a woman because she looks
Straight in their eyes with mournful, trustful gaze,
And lips like innocence, all gentleness.
Your Gormflaith could not answer a woman's eyes.
I did not need to read her in a letter ;
I am not woman yet, but I can feel
What untruths are instinctive in my kind,
And how some men desire deceit from us.

So far the drama, though not without a certain pagan brutality, is four-square within the containing walls of poetry—a fine and living piece of literature. How, then, comes it that on the very last page Mr. Bottomley should be willing to dissipate the final effect of a powerful scene by introducing into the death-chamber two prattling beldames, who, coming to lay the dead woman out, croon over her body a squalid ballad about a louse, and plunge the episode into a conclusion of intolerable bathos ? It is in precisely the same spirit that Mr. William Davies paints a richly picturesque portrait of an old seagoing salt, whose memory was packed with the rough stuff of romance, and then tears the picture to pieces in a colophon :

> " A damn bad sailor and a landshark too,
> No good in port or out "—my granddad said.

The disillusionment of such a finish is complete ; it is like a child destroying its sand-castle in a fit of petulance. And the motive is very much the same in both cases, for it has its origin in a freakish desire to shock.

Cleverness is, indeed, the pitfall of the New Poetry. There is no question about the ingenuity with which its varying moods are exploited, its elaborate symbolism evolved, and its sudden, disconcerting effects exploded upon the imagination. Swift, brilliant images break into the field of vision, scatter like rockets, and leave a trail of flying fire behind. But the general impression is momentary ; there are moods and emotions, but no steady current of ideas behind them. Further, in their determination to surprise and even to puzzle at all costs, these young poets are continually forgetting that the first essence of poetry is beauty ; and that, however much you may have observed the world around you, it is impossible to translate your observation into poetry, without the intervention of the spirit of beauty, controlling the vision, and reanimating the idea.

The temptations of cleverness may be insistent, but its risks are equally great : how great indeed will, perhaps, be best indicated by the example of the " Catholic Anthology," which apparently represents the very newest of all the new poetic movements of the day. This strange little volume bears upon its cover a geometrical device, suggesting that the material within holds the same relation to the art of poetry as the work of the Cubist school holds to the art of painting and design. The product of the volume is mainly American in origin, only one or two of the contributors being of indisputably English birth. But it appears here under the auspices of a house associated with some of the best poetry of the younger generation, and is prefaced by a short lyric by Mr. W. B. Yeats, in which that honoured representative of a very different school of inspiration makes bitter fun of scholars and critics, who

> Edit and annotate the lines
> That young men, tossing on their beds,
> Rhymed out in love's despair
> To flatter beauty's ignorant ear.

The reader will not have penetrated far beyond this warning notice before he finds himself in the very stronghold of literary rebellion, if not of anarchy. Mr. Orrick Johns may be allowed to speak for his colleagues, as well as for himself:

> This is the song of youth,
> This is the cause of myself ;
> I knew my father well and he was a fool,
> Therefore will I have my own foot in the path before
> I take a step ;
> I will go only into new lands,
> And I will walk on no plank-walks.
> The horses of my family are wind-broken,
> And the dogs are old,
> And the guns rust ;
> I will make me a new bow from an ash-tree,
> And cut up the homestead into arrows.

And Mr. Ezra Pound takes up the parable in turn, in the same wooden prose, cut into battens:

Come, my songs, let us express our baser passions.
Let us express our envy for the man with a steady
job and no worry about the future.
You are very idle, my songs,
I fear you will come to a bad end.
You stand about the streets. You loiter at the corners
and bus-stops,
You do next to nothing at all.
You do not even express our inner nobility,
You will come to a very bad end.
And I? I have gone half cracked.

It is not for his audience to contradict the poet, who for once may be allowed to pronounce his own literary epitaph. But this, it is to be noted, is the "poetry" that was to say nothing that might not be said "actually in life—under emotion," the sort of emotion that settles down into the banality of a premature decrepitude:

I grow old. . . . I grow old . . .
I shall wear the bottoms of my trousers rolled.
Shall I part my hair behind? Do I dare to eat a
peach?
I shall wear white flannel trousers, and walk upon
the beach.
I have heard the mermaids singing, each to each.
I do not think that they will sing to me.

Here, surely, is the reduction to absurdity of that school of literary licence which, beginning with the declaration

I knew my father well and he was a fool,

naturally proceeds to the convenient assumption

that everything which seemed wise and true to the father must inevitably be false and foolish to the son. Yet, if the fruits of emancipation are to be recognised in the unmetrical, incoherent banalities of these literary " Cubists," the state of Poetry is indeed threatened with anarchy which will end in something worse even than " red ruin and the breaking up of laws." From such a catastrophe the humour, commonsense, and artistic judgment of the best of the new " Georgians " will assuredly save their generation ; nevertheless, a hint of warning may not be altogether out of place. It was a classic custom in the family hall, when the feast was at its height, to display a drunken slave among the sons of the household, to the end that they, being ashamed at the ignominious folly of his gesticulations, might determine never to be tempted into such a pitiable condition themselves. The custom had its advantages ; for the wisdom of the younger generation was found to be fostered more surely by a single example than by a world of homily and precept.

WAR POETRY
(1914-1918)

THE experience of the present war ought surely to have taught believers in prophecy a trenchant lesson. Never in the history of the world can there have been a time when the prophets have proved more consistently wrong ; and nowhere have they wandered further astray than in those doleful predictions which foretold the temporary overthrow of literature and literary interests. In the first months of the war it seemed generally agreed by critics and creative artists alike that the genius of expression itself was doomed to disappear in the immediate future. Works of imagination, we were assured, must cease to trouble the mind of man ; no poetry worthy of the name was likely to be written during the next twenty years. It was a depressing prospect ; but fortunately the prophecy was no sooner uttered than the event asserted its fallacy. A torrent of poetry began at once to pour from the press ; and the voice of criticism found itself obliged to swing round to the opposite pole. The war, we were then told, had become a very forcing-ground of poetry ; it was recreating the poet's heart out of its own fires ; we were face to face with an almost miraculous renaissance of the poetic spirit. This access of enthusiasm has also faded in its turn ; and its wild confidence is shown to have been no less deceptive than the vain depression which preceded it. We are beginning, in short, to arrive at a more equable condition of judgment, and to see things in more accurate perspective.

The time therefore appears propitious for taking stock of the influence which the war has exercised upon contemporary poetry, and, conversely, for considering the contribution which this poetry has of its own initiative made towards an understanding of the true meaning and significance of War. Of the two considerations, the second is likely to prove the more fruitful. For it would seem to be not so much a fact that the war has made poetry, as that poetry has, now for the first time, made War—made it in its own image, with all the tinsel and gaud of tradition stripped away from it; and so made it perhaps that no sincere artist will ever venture again to represent War in those delusive colours with which Art has been too often content to disguise it in the past. From that dual point of view, at any rate, it is proposed in the following pages to consider the best of the war poetry of the last four years, and to attempt to estimate its spiritual effect upon the character of the nation.

It has been widely argued that the war must have been an inspirer of poetry because so many volumes of verse have been published during the last three years, written by young officers who have fallen in active service. It is the war alone, we are asked to assume, that has of its own creative power forced these otherwise "mute, inglorious Miltons" into song. But every one who has owned friends among public-school and University men must know that the impulse to record emotion in verse is one of the commonest attributes of educated adolescence. As a rule these youthful exercises languish in the privacy of the author's bureau ; and it is only the perfectly worthy ambition of bereaved parents, to raise some personal memorial to a dead son, that has recently haled so many of these manly tributes into the light of publicity. Many of them bear witness to very creditable metrical proficiency ; most of them are distinguished by highly meritorious sentiment. But it would be the falsest of compliments to pretend that they make any real addition to the poetry of War. For the most part they record pleasant memories of school and college, breathe a boyish loyalty to grey cloisters and green glades, but touch the essence of life no deeper than is possible to the soldier's honest determination to go out and do his best. Their mental and spiritual attitude to war, in short, is radically conventional ; and they are thus entirely separated from the really significant poetry of the present war, of which the outstanding characteristic is its absolute freedom from convention, demonstrated in an eager, almost passionate determination to picture War as it reveals itself, not to the outsider, but to the enlightened combatant himself.

And here, at the outset, we find ourselves face to face with the differentiating quality of the best new poetry of War. It is written, not by lookers-on, but by the soldiers themselves. The relation between war and poetry, of course, is as old as either war or poetry itself ; and we stand in no need of the picturesque *pastiches* of Sir Walter Scott to remind us of those wandering minstrels who strayed from castle to castle, singing by the fireside of the doughty deeds of dead heroes, to the end that the young men might be stirred to go out and fight, and the maidens' hearts preserved from breaking while their lovers were away. Most of the war poetry of the past has been the legitimate descendant of these glib eulogists, of whom the first thing to remember is that their whole business is to encourage and to praise, to set romance twittering among the leaves—in short, to tell noble lies about War, that the purpose of the country may be served. Poetry, in fact, has to plead guilty to misrepresenting War, in the cause either of politics or of art—of misrepresenting it as something intrinsically splendid, beautiful, and inspiring. It has persistently confused the issue with the process. Splendid things are done in war, of course ; but they are the issue of war, not its process.

For the mere process of warfare is indisputably a vile, inhuman, devilish abomination, plunged in squalor and filth. It is approached through seas of mud, and pursued amid vermin and all uncleanness. It degrades the body of man ; more than that, it would destroy his very soul itself, were it not for the divine fire that burns at the heart of humanity, and consumes even the weapons of war in the white heat of its truth. And in the present war, when, for the first time since the nation became articulate, fighting has ceased to be the business of a professional class, and has become perforce the bitter duty of the whole manhood of the race, we have had something approaching its true meaning revealed to us in poetry; not because war had any virtue in it that could "make a poet out of a man," but simply because the poet has himself turned soldier, and concentrated upon the ugly and monotonous business of war the keen searchlight of interpretation. The professional soldier is inevitably an unimaginative product; of all classes of the community, he is, perhaps, most completely the victim of tradition. His "not to reason why"; his, in the very nature of things, to do what he is told, and to do it as quickly and as effectually as possible. But, now that war has ceased to be the concern of a professional class, its secrets have been revealed to the world at large. And so, for the first time, we have had the clear lights of intellect and interpretation playing upon the battlefield; and, whatever may be thought of the gain or loss to poetry, there can at least be no question about the extraordinary actuality of this new presentment, about its sincerity, or about the arresting revelation which it affords of the evil and the horror of modern warfare between civilised communities.

The contrast is the more vivid because of the high ideals and the exalted purpose with which the yoke of battle was at first accepted by the nation at large. It has been repeated so often as to have grown tedious that no nation ever entered upon war with a cleaner conscience than Britain in the summer of 1914. And repetition does not dull the edge of that truth; it is indisputably true. No one could accuse Mr. Thomas Hardy for example, of sentimentalising a situation of this kind. If there had been an atom of false pretence about it, his searching gaze would have tracked it down in its secret corner. But for once, as the drums are heard in the village street, the old poet is stirred out of his cynicism, and stands as it were, to attention at the window in the dim light of the early dawn, proud of his fellow-countrymen, and confident in their cause :

What of the faith and fire within us
  Men who march away
  Ere the barn-cocks say
  Night is growing gray,
To hazards whence no tears can win us ?
What of the faith and fire within us
  Men who march away ? . . .

In our heart of hearts believing
  Victory crowns the just,
  And that braggarts must
  Surely bite the dust,
March we to the field ungrieving,
In our heart of hearts believing
  Victory crowns the just.

This sense of a just cause, almost of a sacred crusade, may be said to have inspired all the war poetry written during the closing months of 1914. In Mr. Laurence Binyon's rich and high-hearted " For the Fallen " it is presented as the one sure amulet of consolation.

With proud thanksgiving, a mother for her children,
England mourns for her dead across the sea.
Flesh of her flesh they were, spirit of her spirit,
Fallen in the cause of the free. . . .

Something of the same sentiment, too, broods over the harvest-fields in Mr. John Masefield's

" August, 1914," linking to the present sacrifice all those sons of the soil who in the past have left home and loved ones and hope, for the sake of an immortal dream of freedom :

> And died (uncouthly, most) in foreign lands
> For some idea but dimly understood
> Of an English city never built by hands,
> Which love of England prompted and made good.

This was the universal sentiment of our poetry at the outset of the war ; but it was a sentiment which, in the nature of things, would scarcely survive the insistent claim of personality. In particular, it could not be expected to survive the ordeal of individual experience. It was detached, remote—the sentiment, in a word, of the onlooker. It was once more the true descendant of the old ballad poetry, made by men who stood outside the fiery trial of battle. It philosophised the situation, but it did not embody it realistically.

Now, as it happened, the chief tendency in English verse for several years before the outbreak of the war had been a tendency towards crude realism, finding its inspiration in themes which had hitherto, perhaps, been considered impossible to the idealising spirit of poetry. The younger generation, perceiving that the idyllic school of verse had inevitably exhausted its capacities, appeared to have set its heart upon proving that no subject lies intrinsically outside the limits of poetic treatment, and that poetry can draw to its service, and ennoble by its interpretation, even the most uncouth and hideous circumstance. The war, therefore, may be said to have afforded our young realists the richest possible opportunity for concentrating their art upon the vital moments of life and death. It was an opportunity at once pictorial and psychological. Its appeal was equally to the eye and to the heart; and it was immediately accepted with the eager frankness characteristic of our younger writers, and with the prevalent determination to speak the truth about the ugly things of life, and to strip suffering bare of all concealing veils of sentimentality and pretence. The work of revelation has been undertaken with untrammelled honesty; and its completion raises a very important problem. How far, we must ask, can poetry proceed in the vivid portrayal of death and destruction, and yet remain what poetry must always be, if it is to be worthy of its traditions—a spiritual interpretation of the soul of man in conflict with his environment?

The first stage, at any rate, of the poet's initiation in the school of war brings with it no difficulty at all; it is purely and intimately introspective. It follows tradition with unfaltering step; and the first change to be observed is a rather startling retrogression from the universal to the purely personal point of view. It is comparatively easy for the onlooker to be eloquent in behalf of a cause; but the man who is swept into the field of action becomes, at the first onset, disconcertingly conscious of his own individuality and of his immediate personal risk. The young man trained to an intellectual life, with the plans for his future career plain before him, can scarcely break with so many associations unmoved by a sense of sacrifice; and the first poems to be written by soldier-poets were almost inevitably touched by a certain irresistible sense of self-pity. Rupert Brooke's sonnet "The Soldier" is the natural utterance of a young man who is leaving behind him everything that made life worth living, and who, faced by the prospect of an untimely death, seeks his consolation in bringing the future into some sort of permanent relation with the past. Wherever he falls, he will carry with him some spirit of his home, some tribute to his training, some memorial of his love. And other poems, like Mr. Robert Nichols's "Farewell," and the "Into Battle" of Julian Grenfell, are inspired by the same vague uncertainty, the same tremulous trust that a man may be remembered as having shown the courage which all the education of his youth was designed to breed.

> They shall not say I went with heavy heart :
> Heavy I am, but soon I shall be free,
> I love them all, but oh, I now depart
> A little sadly, strangely, fearfully,
> As one who goes to try a mystery.

And again :

> The kestrel hovering by day,
>   And the little owls that call by night,
> Bid him be swift and keen as they,
>   As keen of ear, as swift of sight.
>
> The blackbird sings to him, "Brother, brother,
>   If this be the last song you shall sing,
> Sing well, for you may not sing another ;
>   Brother, sing."

In these first moments of solitude it is perhaps

inevitable that a man should be thinking of himself, but the mood passes with extraordinary rapidity; and the next change in the poet's attitude to War can be traced in almost every one of the young writers who have actually been into the front lines. The sense of a cause vanishes; the sense of self vanishes; and over all spreads an impenetrable, absorbing prepossession that War is after all merely another form of toiling, moiling business, beset with detail, loaded with obligation, in which the individual soldier is of no more significance than the proverbial cog in a vast mass of labouring machinery.

Men, as Mr. Gilbert Frankau sees them clearly, have become the slaves of the guns.

> These are our masters, the slim
>   Grim muzzles that irk in the pit;
> That chafe for the rushing of wheels,
>   For the teams plunging madly to bit
> As the gunners swing down to unkey,
>   For the trails sweeping half-circle-right,
> For the six breech-blocks clashing as one
>   To a target viewed clear on the sight—
> Dun masses, the shells search and tear
>   Into fragments that bunch as they run—
> For the hour of the red battle-harvest,
>   The dream of the slaves of the gun.

In these Kiplingesque lines the creak of the machine has practically drowned the voice of poetry altogether; but the authentic note sounds less uncertainly in Mr. Robert Nichols's "On the Way Up."

> The battery grides and jingles,
> Mile succeeds to mile;

Tradition and Change

Shaking the noonday sunshine,
The guns lunge out awhile
And then are still awhile.

We amble along the highway;
The reeking, powdery dust
Ascends and cakes our faces,
With a striped, sweaty crust.

Under the still sky's violet
The heat throbs in the air . . .
The white road's dusty radiance
Assumes a dark glare.

With a head hot and heavy,
And eyes that cannot rest,
And a black heart burning
In a stifled breast,

I sit in the saddle,
I feel the road unroll,
And keep my senses straightened
Towards to-morrow's goal.

Until

Nearer and ever nearer,
My body tired but tense
Hovers 'twixt vague pleasure
And tremulous confidence.

Arms to have and to use them,
And a soul to be made
Worthy if unworthy;
If afraid, unafraid.

To endure for a little,
To endure and have done:
Men I love about me,
Over me the sun!

And should at last suddenly
Fly the speeding death :
The four great quarters of heaven
Receive this little breath.

These pieces, which are grouped together in Mr. Osborn's suggestive anthology,* under the general title of "The Approach," may be said to bridge the gulfs that separate the three stages in the poet's initiation. In the first, where the battery has halted by the wayside, a sudden paroxysm of fear attacks the soldier. For a moment he is absorbed once more in himself. In the next, he has become a part of the machinery of war; the battery itself is the unit, and community of task the whole duty of life. In the third, community of task has opened out into human sympathy. "Men I love about me!" The machinery of war has revealed itself as composed of an infinity of human atoms, every one with a history, and a significance of its own. The man has passed out of himself into the heart of others; and, while life is seen to be made up of an endless sequence of little things, nothing in life, now so perpetually at odds with death, appears to be unworthy of care and consideration. This is, perhaps, the one and only helpful lesson that war brings home to the common soldier's heart, and it is instilled in a variety of different guises.

The life of the soldier lumbers along, revealing itself in broken glimpses through a mist of grey monotony. One thing which home-keeping age finds it difficult to realise is the interminable dulness which slowly settles down upon what

* "The Muse in Arms." Edited by E. B. Osborn.

once promised to be an heroic campaign. There are stretches of irksome inaction, during which the mind labours to reconcile itself with its uncongenial occupation. Weary detail, uninspired vigil, perpetual repetition of duties only half understood, throw the mind back upon itself and feed it with memory. In such lonely hours the impressions of the past become importunate, and flashes of the old life penetrate through the most unlikely environment. Wyndham Tennant describes this poignantly in " Home Thoughts in Laventie."

> Hungry for spring, I bent my head,
> The perfume fanned my face,
> And all my soul was dancing
> In that little lovely place,
> Dancing with a measured step from wrecked and shattered towns
> Away—upon the Downs.
>
> I saw green banks of daffodils,
> Slim poplars in the breeze,
> Great tan-brown hares in gusty March
> A-courting on the leas ;
> And meadows with their glittering streams, and silver scurrying dace,
> Home—what a perfect place !

And gradually the very contrast between the broad calm of the past and the infinite restlessness of the present draws the man out of himself into some sort of philosophic resignation.

> Here there are the great things, life and death, and danger,
> All I ever dreamed of in the days that used to be,
> Comrades and good-fellowship, the soul of an army,
> But oh, it is the little things that take the heart of me.

For all we knew of old, for little things and lovely,
We bow us to a greater life beyond our hope or fear,
To bear its heavy burdens, endure its toils unheeding,
Because of all the little things so distant and so dear.*

Many of the soldier-poets recur naturally to their school-days, fighting old battles over again on field and in class-room. In this context in particular there emerges the new type of student-in-arms, the bookman, the classical scholar, the meditative yet virile public-school product, bred on good literature and good sport, who carries Homer in his haversack, and dreams of Achilles in the trenches. Of this type a brave and stimulating example is afforded by Charles Hamilton Sorley, whose imagination seems to flood the squalid present with the picturesque heroism of the past. He carries the sunlight of ancient Sparta into the drab, drenched flats of Flanders, and sees the end of conflict in an ideal city of dreams, built " half in heaven " and half upon the windy Marlborough downs.

Soon, O soon, I do not doubt it,
With the body or without it,
We shall all come tumbling down
To our old wrinkled red-capped town.
Perhaps the road up Ilsley way,
The old ridge-track, will be my way.
High up among the sheep and sky,
Look down on Wantage, passing by,
And see the smoke from Swindon town ;
And then full left at Liddington.
Where the four winds of heaven meet
The earth-blest traveller to greet,

* "A Highland Regiment." By E. A. Mackintosh.

And then my face is toward the south,
There is a singing on my mouth :
Away to rightward I descry
My Barbury ensconced in sky,
Far underneath the Ogbourne twins,
And at my feet the thyme and whins,
The grasses with their little crowns
Of gold, the lovely Aldbourne downs,
And that old signpost (well I knew
That crazy signpost, arms askew,
Old mother of the four grass ways).
And then my mouth is dumb with praise,
For, past the wood and chalkpit tiny,
A glimpse of Marlborough ἐρατεινή !
So I descend beneath the rail
To warmth and welcome and wassail.

Dreams like these mingle inextricably with the rough-and-ready consolations of companionship. Life has run to waste in a tangle of things imagined and things seen ; in the confusion of values the mind grasps at any kind of respite or relief, and, when the pressure is relaxed, and the company is back in billets, as in Captain Charles Scott-Moncrieff's cheery ballad, the simplest, silliest jests have a savour, merely because they help the soldier to forget the perpetually-brooding cloud that lies ahead. The very measure of life changes, returning to a world of jingle.

Mustn't think we don't mind when a chap gets laid out,
They've taken the best of us, never a doubt ;
But with life pretty busy and death rather near
We've no time for regret any more than for fear.

. . . . . .

You may talk of the Ritz or the Carlton (Mayfair)
And maintain that they keep you in luxury there:
If you've laid for six weeks on a water-logged plain,
Here's the acme of comfort, in billets again.

Here is no longer, it must be recognised, any dream of heroism, of a cause or a crusade, of broidered banners or a watchword. As dreams merge into reality, men, and men alone, become the material of life; and through the machinery of war the young officer is drawn into sympathy with all who are part and parcel of the same machine. There is no sentimentality about it. The communion of endurance makes them all kin.

Mr. Siegfried Sassoon, perhaps, has expressed better than any one else this emancipation of the soldier's heart from the taint of selfishness. It is the animating spirit of his vivid little piece of realism, "In the Pink." The young subaltern, who records the impression, has entered into the very soul of the private, as he scrawls a letter home to his rustic sweetheart, comforting her with consolations which his own environment belies.

So Davies wrote: "This leaves me in the pink."
Then scrawled his name: "Your loving sweet-
heart, Willie,"
With crosses for a hug. He'd had a drink
Of rum and tea; and, though the barn was chilly,
For once his blood ran warm; he'd pay to spend.
Winter was passing; soon the year would mend.

He couldn't sleep that night. Stiff in the dark
He groaned and thought of Sundays at the farm,
When he'd go out as cheerful as a lark

In his best suit to wander arm-in-arm
With brown-eyed Gwen, and whisper in her ear
The simple, silly things she liked to hear.

And then he thought: to-morrow night we trudge
Up to the trenches, and my boots are rotten.
Five miles of stodgy clay and freezing sludge,
And everything but wretchedness forgotten.
To-night he's in the pink; but soon he'll die.
And still the war goes on; *he* don't know why.

The war goes on, moreover, through a panorama of cruel inequalities, which serve to strip militarism of its last vestiges of glamour. David, as Captain Graves reminds us, no longer triumphs picturesquely over his towering giant. Brute force is stronger than the human heart.

> (God's eyes are dim, His ears are shut.)
> One cruel backhand sabre cut—
> "I'm hit! I'm killed!" young David cries,
> Throws blindly forward, chokes . . . and dies.
> And look, spike-helmeted, grey, grim,
> Goliath straddles over him.

The inevitable response to such experiences is, on the one hand, an honest, deep, and undemonstrative sympathy with the men who suffer; and, on the other, an intolerant contempt for the false sentiment with which ignorant people at home so fatuously invest the horrors of war. Sometimes, as in the late Lieut. Mackintosh's touching "In Memoriam," the sentiment wavers towards an almost feminine air of protectiveness. The young officer pictures himself as filling a parental relation to his men, losing something of his own life with every man who falls:

Oh, never will I forget you,
My men that trusted me,
More my sons than your fathers',
For they would only see
The little helpless babies
And the young men in their pride.
They could not see you dying,
And hold you while you died.

The same feeling, revealed in a scene of the finest dramatic quality, animates Mr. Robert Nichols's " Comrades," where the dying subaltern, Gates, struggles back to the trenches, mortally wounded, every movement an accentuation of his suffering, out of sheer determination to die among the men for whom he is responsible:

Inch by inch he fought, breathless and mute,
Dragging his carcase like a famished brute. . . .
His head was hammering and his eyes were dim,
A bloody sweat seemed to ooze out of him
And freeze along his spine . . . then he'd lie still
Before another effort of his will
Took him one nearer yard.

. . . .

The parapet was reached.
He could not rise to it. A look-out screeched,
" Mr. Gates ! "
Three figures in one breath
Leaped up. Two figures fell in toppling death ;
And Gates was lifted in. " Who's hit ? " said he.
" Timmins and Jones." " Why did they that for me ?
I'm gone already ! " Gently they laid him prone
And silently watched.
He twitched. They heard him moan,
" Why for me ? " His eyes roamed round and none replied.
" I see it was alone I should have died."

They shook their heads. Then, " Is the doctor here ? "
" He's comin', sir, he's hurryin', no fear."
" No good . . . Lift me." They lifted him.
He smiled and held his arms out to the dim,
And in a moment passed beyond their ken,
Hearing him whisper, " O my men, my men ! "

So powerful indeed does the immediate influence of a common life become that by degrees all other associations fade before its white-hot vehemence. The present detaches the soldier altogether from the past. Home, love, even the one loved above all, are forgotten. Tenderness seems like a far-away memory ; the soldier's concern is with the soldier's life alone :

> Faces cheerful, full of whimsical mirth,
> Lined by the wind, burned by the sun ;
> Bodies enraptured by the abounding earth,
> As whose children, brothers we are and one.
>
> And any moment may descend hot death
> To shatter limbs ! pulp, tear and blast
> Belovéd soldiers who love rough life and breath
> Not less for dying faithful to the last.
>
> O the fading eyes, the griméd face turned bony,
> Oped, black, gushing mouth, fallen head,
> Failing pressure of a held hand, shrunk and stony !
> O sudden spasm, release of the dead !
>
> Was there love once ? I have forgotten her.
> Was there grief once ? grief still is mine.
> O loved, living, dying, heroic soldier,
> All, all my joy, my grief, my love, are thine !

To those whose life has for months been riddled with visions such as these it is no wonder that a return to home, and the sudden recognition of its false sentiment and falser humour should assault the mind with the sting of intolerable resentment. The old, familiar glosses upon war are indeed effectually held up to scorn by our young realists. Mr. Siegfried Sassoon's "They," with its bitter arraignment of episcopal platitude, is well-balanced by the same poet's almost vindictive cameo of a London music-hall in war-time :

The House is crammed ; tier beyond tier they grin
And cackle at the Show, while prancing ranks
Of harlots shrill the chorus, drunk with din ;
"We're sure the Kaiser loves the dear old Tanks!"

I'd like to see a tank come down the stalls,
Lurching to rag-time tunes, or "Home, sweet
 Home,"—
And there'd be no more jokes in Music-halls
To mock the riddled corpses round Bapaume.

The reflective attitude of modern poetry to war can hardly go further. Sympathy has merged itself in a furious detestation of all those false pretences which in the past have presented the military spirit as a sort of enclosed garden of the poets' fantasy. The men who have seen the thing as it is have left the rest of us in no sort of doubt upon one indisputable fact. The poetry of the future will hardly venture to sentimentalise an experience which can prompt so sincere and so overwhelming an indignation. And indeed it is already to be noted that among those poets also, who have not themselves made personal trial of war, a new and restrained spirit may be recognised.

The truth has come home to the civilian no less than to the soldier. Mr. Harold Monro's picture of the family gathering the night before the soldier returns to the front labours under no vain illusion with regard to the compensating glory of loss. Every moment, viewed from the stay-at-home's standpoint, is heavy with apprehension ; every tick of the clock is like the warning of a death-watch. Suffering has become personal, intimate, homely, as all deep suffering always is. And when the news of loss comes home, as in Mr. J. C. Squire's exquisitely poignant poem " To a Bull-Dog," it is no longer decorated with conventional comfort, but accepted, simply and honestly, for the devastating thing it is. The dog and one of his masters are left alone ; the other master has fallen at the front. The poet addresses his dumb companion:

When summer comes again,
  And the long sunsets fade,
We shall have to go on playing the feeble game for two
  That since the war we've played.

And though you run expectant as you always do
  To the uniforms we meet,
You'll never find Willy among all the soldiers
  In even the longest street,

Nor in any crowd ; yet, strange and bitter thought,
  Even now were the old words said,
If I tried the old trick and said " Where's Willy ? "
  You would quiver and lift your head,

And your brown eyes would look to ask if I was
    serious,
  And wait for the word to spring.
Sleep undisturbed : I shan't say *that* again,
  You innocent old thing.

Simple, direct pathos could scarcely be expressed in simpler, more direct phrase ; and yet the metrical scheme of the poem is full of subtlety, rising on the wave of the long line, just as the thought rises in intensity, and sinking back into repose in the short. Expression seems to be matched quite perfectly with thought ; and the sentiment, purged of all self-pity and protestation, becomes almost intolerably sincere.

Sincerity, indeed, is the essence of the light with which the poetry of the last four years has slowly and increasingly flooded the crowded theatre of war. The quotations which we have given may surely speak for themselves. They must be acknowledged as presenting a broad panorama of the soldier's life, from the day he leaves England until the hour of his death upon the field of honour ; and their outstanding virtue is the penetration with which they probe to the essential spirit of warfare. Springing from various and diverse temperaments, they illustrate in turn the honest soldier's fear of fear, his pilgrimage from self-consciousness to altruism, his absorption into the machinery of war, and his gradual appreciation of that complex machine as a collection of human characters, each individual and all interacting, combining at last into a unity in which self is merged absolutely in a sense of common purpose and general obligation. The comparison of this poetry with the poetry of any other war in the history of the world can hardly fail to reassure the critic that, so far as the spiritual interpretation of war is concerned, the poets have risen manfully to their opportunity, and have abundantly justified the claim to sincerity and directness which appears to be the staple ambition of modern poetry, whatever its theme and occupation.

So far, it will be noted, we have been considering the function of Poetry in offering a representation of War, psychologically and through its influence upon the soldier's mind; there remains to be considered the value of the material which War in its turn has offered to poetry, from the actual or realistic standpoint. And here, we believe, there has been a general tendency to overrate the value of the contribution. It has been claimed, for instance, that in the sister-art of painting the war has furnished artists with inspiration of the liveliest possibility. Can this be said with equal truth of Poetry? It seems very doubtful; and in any case the ground was ready-made for Poetry long before War had been dreamt of outside the impenetrable councils of Berlin. In the years immediately preceding the war there had been, as we have already noted, a growing fashion in English verse to seek crude and violent subjects for poetry; and this fashion was perilously fostered by the popular success of such realistic exercises as Mr. John Masefield's "The Everlasting Mercy" and "The Widow in the Bye-Street," which may perhaps be said to display the method to its most effectual advantage.

The fashion was already exhausting itself

before the autumn of 1914, but it has been adopted by a few experimentalists in an attempt to represent the outward aspects of War, condensed and vitalised to a single vivid and entirely external impression. It is noticeable, however, that the attempt has not been so much encouraged by those who had already affected this particular kind of realism, as accepted by others in a sort of faint discipleship. Such poems as Mr. Masefield himself has devoted to the war have been almost entirely psychological and interpretative ; and of the older of the Georgian poets it has been left to Mr. Gibson to whittle poetry down to its barest core, in the effort to present a keen and undecorated outline of fact. It cannot be said that the experiment is altogether fortunate, despite the keen hardness of the workmanship :

> This bloody steel
>   Has killed a man.
> I heard him squeal
>   As on I ran.
>
> He watched me come
>   With wagging head.
> I pressed it home,
>   And he was dead.
>
> Though clean and clear
>   I've wiped the steel,
> I still can hear
>   That dying squeal.

Or again :

> I watched it oozing quietly
>   Out of the gaping gash.
> The lads thrust on to victory
>   With lunge and curse and crash. . . .

The lads thrust on to victory,
   With lunge and crash and shout.
I lay and watched, as quietly
   His life was running out.

Nothing could be simpler or more self-contained, and yet it must be confessed that such experiments as these are failures. They fail, because they are concerned exclusively with external facts ; imagination has not got to work upon them ; the poet's art has not even made the effort of fusing the fact with the idea. And the same is true of Mr. Robert Nichols's "Assault," an elaborate attempt to give instant and compelling expression to the sights and sounds of onslaught, which nevertheless falls completely short of the true, interpretative service of poetry to life :

I hear my whistle shriek
Between teeth set ;
I fling an arm up,
Scramble up the grime
Over the parapet !

I'm up. Go on.
Something meets us.
Head down into the storm that greets us.

A wail !
Lights. Blurr.
Gone.
On, on. Lead. Lead. Hail.
Spatter. Whirr. Whirr.

The true test of poetry must always be the test of reading aloud. Unless a poem can bear recitation, its workmanship is condemned. And to read Mr. Nichols's " Assault " aloud is to be persuaded of a creaking chain of artistic improprieties, which strain vehemently towards effect, only to end in incoherence :

> Ha ! Ha ! Bunched figures waiting.
> Revolver levelled : quick !
> Flick ! Flick !
> Red as blood.
> Germans. Germans.
> Good ! Oh, good !
>
> Cool madness.

This is neither metre nor *vers libre*. It has no form or true proportion ; the fever of war has infected it, and left it void.

The fact is, of course, that Poetry can only be produced when imagination has fused fact ; and that this fusion is possible, even to emphatically realistic verse, is proved by the impressive success of Captain Robert Graves's " It's a Queer Time," where the poet reproduces, with provocative fidelity, that familiar state of mind under which a man is conscious of acting with his bodily functions in one world, while he is living with his brain in another. Past and present are commingled in a riot of confusion.

> You're charging madly at them yelling " Fag ! "
> When somehow something gives and your feet drag.
> You fall and strike your head ; yet feel no pain
> And find . . . you're digging tunnels through the hay
> In the Big Barn, 'cause it's a rainy day.
> O springy hay, and lovely beams to climb !
> You're back in the old sailor-suit again.
> It's a queer time.

Or you'll be dozing safe in your dug-out—
A great roar—the trench shakes and falls about—
You're struggling, gasping, struggling, then . . .
    hullo !
Elsie comes tripping gaily down the trench.
Hanky to nose—that lyddite makes a stench—
Getting her pinafore all over grime.
Funny ! because she died ten years ago !
    It's a queer time.

This realism of the intellectual aspect of War, as contrasted with the merely material realism of lamp-black and lightning, has indeed afforded poetry a new scope for the imagination ; and particularly in the work of Captain Graves, Mr. Siegfried Sassoon, and some of that of Mr. Robert Nichols, it has produced verse of a quality which could not, perhaps, have found inspiration at all in times of peace and contentment. But it will be noted at once that it is a realism which depends, for its very essence, upon a transcendental interpretation. The war, in other words, has only furnished poetry with material, when Poetry has brought to its aid a secret interpretation which is, in effect, the very antithesis of War itself. The concomitants of War are noise, squalor, filth—the worst antagonists of the poet's art. So long as the poet is content with merely superficial pictures of noise, squalor, and filth, War affords him no adequate opportunity. Its entire world is too barren, too hard, too hideous to issue in poetry. Even Captain Graves goes artistically wrong with his bloated portrait of the dead Boche. The image is starkly repellent ; imagination has failed to light it up. But directly imagination gets to work, it finds the soul beneath the surface, and then at last Poetry issues from the union.

A comparison of the spirit of this new poetry with that of the generation which preceded it would seem to suggest that War has most certainly not been without its purging influence upon the artistic soul of youth. For the new poetry is honest; it is strong; and it is often very beautiful. Decadence, at any rate, has vanished; triviality is no more; eccentricity has almost disappeared. And with these inadequate tricks of manner there has also disappeared a certain narrowness or selfishness of outlook upon the world around. The old formula of youth in the Ibsen period, the formula that clamoured for every man to live out his own life after his own fashion, has yielded before a realisation that no man's life can belong to himself, even for a moment; and that, when all is said and done, the individual life is of very little concern to the world at large. Sentimentality has been most healthily lived down; there is an almost universal distrust of conventional consolation. Religion, perhaps, has lost the vigour of its hold upon the imagination, and one can trace very little faith in any survival of personality after death. But a larger and an austerer hope still finds the dead inseparable from every haunt of old association.

Walking through trees to cool my heat and pain,
I know that David's with me here again.
All that is simple, happy, strong he is.
Caressingly I stroke
Rough bark of the friendly oak.
A brook goes bubbling by: the voice is his.

Turf burns with pleasant smoke :
I laugh at chaffinch and at primroses.
All that is simple, happy, strong, he is.
Over the whole wood in a little while
Breaks his slow smile.

We end, then, with the conclusion that Poetry, in spite of many tribulations, is well justified of its supreme ordeal. It has gone down into the darkness, and has carried light in its hand. Our young men, indeed, have grown old, as befits those who have been face to face with death. It may be true that the war has made Stoics of our Hedonists, but in the process it has also made men. And, being men, they have not feared to speak the truth about the bitter discipline under which they have emerged into manhood. It is a terrible truth, wounding the speaker and the hearer alike ; but it is a truth that may yet help to set free the soul of humanity for nobler victories in the years of peace.

STEPHEN PHILLIPS

TO die at fifty, an age when the intellectual and creative faculties should naturally be at their richest and ripest, and yet to have lived long enough to outlast the hey-day of one's success and reputation—this is a hard fate for a poet who has seen himself acclaimed with all the titles of literary immortality. It is an even harder fate when success has come, as it were, spontaneously, without pursuit or importunity. The man who has had to wait long for recognition, enduring perhaps years of uncertainty and disappointment, is already armed against the vicissitudes of fortune. What has happened before he knows may happen again; meanwhile the years of sunlight are sweet and commendable. But the man who achieves fame almost at his first throw is less equipped to face disillusionment. Success that comes easily seems certain to be easily retained; and when it is perceived to be slowly filtering away, the experience can hardly fail to be exceedingly bitter. The injustice of Fortune appears the more intolerable for its unexpectedness. And the brighter the triumphs may have been, the darker will prove their eclipse.

Some such experience, it is to be feared, helped to cloud the last days of Stephen Phillips, whose premature death brought to a close many bright hopes and expectations. Few men in our generation have achieved success so instantaneously; very few contemporary poets have enjoyed such high praise. The criticisms collected at the end of his books compare or contrast him, to his own high credit, with half the masters of the poetic and dramatic arts. Dante, Marlowe, Shakespeare, Milton, Webster, Chapman, Racine, Dumas, Sardou, Tennyson, Rossetti, Landor—these are a few of the names brought forward in tribute to decorate the singing-robes of the author of " Marpessa." Nor did the praise come from any inconsiderable quarter. These rich comparisons are signed by some of the most distinguished literary judges of the day ; certain of them, indeed, by judges from whom it was generally difficult for a young reputation to exact approval. Churton Collins, for example, was certainly not the man to grow enthusiastic over every " new thing " that might loom above the literary horizon. He more often confronted novelty from the peak of Ebal than of Gerizim. Yet it was Churton Collins who alligned Stephen Phillips with Dante and Milton, and declared that " no poet has made his *début* with a volume which is at once of such extraordinary merit and so rich in promise." These are glowing eulogies ; but they, and all their like, did no more than reflect faithfully the prevailing critical enthusiasm of the time. Twenty years ago Stephen Phillips stood out conspicuously in the public eye as one of the two or three poets in whose care the future of English poetry might safely be permitted to repose. The approval of the critics had even been endorsed at the counters of the booksellers. For Stephen Phillips was not only talked about ; his books were bought and read. For ten years or more he presented the rare figure of a poet whom critical and uncritical alike appreciate. And yet upon the day of his death there was scarcely a single obituary notice which did not adopt a half-veiled but unmistakable attitude of apology. For in the meanwhile the sudden change had intervened. Critical fashion, popular taste, the national standard of judgment, each and all of these constituents of fame had somehow or other shifted their ground. The poet, who had once perhaps been over-praised, was now unquestionably under-estimated. The public had grown tired and ungrateful; it no longer did him justice. And the critics, reasonably discontented with his later work, had somehow forgotten, or regretted, their earlier confidence. It seems hard; and it is not altogether sound. Perhaps its very hardship may excuse an attempt to re-adjust the balance, and to recall the true qualities and real achievements of a career which once set many lights ablaze, and echoed to many half-forgotten but memorable plaudits. For there are some of us, among his earliest admirers in the golden days, who would be unwilling to let our memories of him close without some kindly tribute of gratitude and esteem.

I

The bare incidents of the poet's life afford little material of interest to the biographer. He was the son of an eminent divine, and was born at Summertown, in the suburbs of Oxford. He went to school at Stratford-on-Avon, and afterwards at Peterborough, where his father was Precentor and Honorary Canon of the Cathedral;

and it is said that the boy's love of poetry was first aroused in his fifteenth year by hearing his mother read "Christabel" aloud. He was intended for the Civil Service, and was working at a well-known crammer's in Garrick Street when his passion for the stage broke loose, and he threw over all prospects of an official career to join the Shakespearean company of his relative, Sir F. R. Benson. He was not a great success upon the stage. In such parts as Hastings, in "Richard III," Snake in "The School for Scandal," Morocco in "The Merchant of Venice," Sergeant Loupy in "Robert Macaire," Gremio in "The Taming of the Shrew," and King Claudius and the Ghost (on different occasions, of course) in "Hamlet," he proved himself a stiff actor, moving heavily across the stage, and wearing his costume without ease. But he spoke blank verse with a certain sonorous fervour, which rendered his impersonation of The Ghost the best of all his performances.

It will be worth while to consider, in its proper place, the influence which this stage-training exercised upon his own dramatic poetry later on. Undoubtedly the influence was not small. Meanwhile a few years of touring in the provinces exhausted the poet's enthusiasm for an actor's life. He took up a post in an army tutor's, and for six years endured the drudgery of cramming listless young men with ingenious "tips" for examinations. By the end of that time he had published "Marpessa," "Eremus," and "Christ in Hades," and when his collected "Poems" appeared in 1897, and were recognised by the public advertisement of a prize of

£100 offered by *The Academy* for the most important book of the year, their author attracted publicity to such an extent that it was no longer necessary for him to depend upon any outside profession for a living. For his books began to sell by the tens of thousands, actor-managers were at his feet, and the triumphs of His Majesty's and the St. James's Theatres made him the most popular poetic dramatist of our own generation. "Herod" was produced in a storm of applause in 1900, and "Paolo and Francesca" (published in 1899) achieved a tremendous success on the stage in 1902. There followed "Ulysses" and "Nero," upon which Sir Herbert Tree lavished all the splendour of his elaborate stage-management. These were the years of harvesting, and a triumphant time they were for the poet's welfare. It is small wonder that his imagination flourished and fed upon itself, to the inevitable misfortune of his genius. For there are few things harder for the human soul to sustain with equanimity than a sudden and universal popularity.

II

To a great popular success various elements are needed, but not least among them is the advantage of opportunity. The genius who appears at the right moment has his way made plain before him; and there can be no doubt that Stephen Phillips was exceedingly fortunate in the time in which he began to write. The years immediately following Tennyson's death were great years for the young poets. For a whole generation the Tennysonian tradition had kept

English poetry stagnant. The example and influence of Tennyson were so predominant that almost every beginner started in his footsteps. Nevertheless signs had not been wanting that the world was growing restless and discontented under the artistic autocracy of Farringford. For some time before Tennyson's death any poetic movement that broke away from his influence had been eagerly welcomed and acclaimed: Swinburne was an inspiration; William Morris a trumpet-call. And now that these two rebellious talents were no longer novelties, in the very hour of uncertainty which followed the break-up of the Tennysonian era, Stephen Phillips stepped firmly into the limelight, thundering out a new form of blank verse, and of the heroic couplet, which was not Tennyson's, nor Swinburne's, nor Morris's, but born of the house of Marlowe, and descended through the line of the Spasmodists, a rich, sensuous, overloaded, but irresistibly powerful medium, so strong and insidious as to take the fancy captive in a mist of eloquence.

> O wine of the world, the odour and gold of it!"

It is not surprising that such glorious rhetoric should have carried us all off our feet!

Looking back now, however, when time has mellowed first impressions, it seems strange that we should none of us have recognised that, however much the author of "Christ in Hades" had imported into contemporary verse of fire and fervour, of romanticism and spirituality, he was still, as a matter of fact, very modestly restricted in the technical resources of his art. Of metrical variety he had almost none. All his best work was done in blank verse, or in the heroic couplet. The lyrical innovations of Swinburne and the Pre-Raphaelites might never have been heard of, for any effect they exercised upon Stephen Phillips's prosody. He began to write in a period of feverish lyrical experiment, but experiment and innovation had no interest for him whatever. Apparently he lacked the lyric impulse altogether. His long apprenticeship to the recitation of blank verse had left him careless of any other vehicle of expression. His stage experience no doubt, was responsible to some extent for this limitation, but the few lyrics upon which the poet adventured do not encourage the idea that he could ever have achieved much as a singer. His ear was not sensitive, nor his sense of melody acute.

Indeed, there was one respect in which his ear was so much at variance with the prevailing taste that he soon found himself involved in a vigorous controversy with the critics. Since the days of Pope considerable liberties had been taken with the ten-syllabled line, and Dr. Johnson, who believed that English prosody could scarcely advance beyond the metallic formality of "The Rape of the Lock," would have been amazed (and perhaps disgusted) at the dactyls and anapaests with which Swinburne had relieved the monotony of the heroic couplet. Phillips went a step further, or perhaps it should more correctly be said, took a step backward, and sheltering himself under the mantle of Milton, introduced an occasional trochee in place of an iambus, for the sake of a desirable variety. Some of these lines offended contemporary taste not a little :

> Gentle and all injured. Art thou a God ? . . .
> My bloom faded, and waning light of eyes . . .
> And I in silence wondered at sorrow. . . .
> O all fresh out of beautiful sunlight. . . .

Lines likes these were naturally difficult to reconcile with the Tennysonian tradition ; but Mr. William Archer and Mr. James Douglas charging into the lists, found themselves confronted with the sturdy lance of the present Poet Laureate, shod at the fighting end with plentiful Miltonic authority. The controversy would scarcely be possible to-day, when the younger men care little for tradition, and such verses as :

> All the enginery of going on sea

or

> Of a wild vinegar into our sheathéd marrows

pass current for respectable workmanship. But there will still remain a few of us to whom

> O all fresh out of beautiful sunlight

will stand as a stumbling block, defying the ear. And it is by no means certain that the last word is with the innovators.

In any case, this small trochaic licence represents the limit of Stephen Phillips's innovations ; for the rest, he depended from the outset upon a powerful theme rather than upon a lyrical treatment, and in his choice of themes he was almost as fortunate as in the opportunity of exploiting them. Viewed historically, he seems to have joined hands with the last of the romanticists, and with the first of the realists. He had not forgotten Tennyson, and yet he anticipated Mr.

John Masefield. The public that was shocked at " The Wife " was not yet ready for " The Widow in the Bye-Street," but the genius that had the courage to describe a woman's sacrifice of her own honour to buy bread for a dying husband was certainly a harbinger of the Georgians. The final touch which brings the dishonoured woman home too late is absolutely in the Masefield vein. The husband is dead, but the child is alive and hungry. The mother is hungry also :

When hunger pained : no thought she had, no care,
She and the child together ate that fare.

The younger realists have drawn no grimmer picture, nor one of a more bitter poignancy.

But we must not flatter ourselves that what first attracted us to Stephen Phillips twenty years ago was his sage prevision of future poetic movements, or our own appreciation of his audacity. As a matter of fact, this audacity was generally regarded with suspicion, and the qualities which made his way were the poet's unfailing sense of a dramatic situation, and the splendid ardour and force with which he developed it. It was not for nothing that the author of " Marpessa " had served his apprenticeship upon the stage, for all his earlier successes were based upon the dramatic value of a single penetrating situation. Take " Marpessa " for example : the choice which is offered to its heroine is essentially dramatic in its appeal—dramatic, and almost theatrical. She is wooed by Apollo and by Idas, a god and a mortal, and she decides in favour of the mortal. The motive of her choice is thoroughly Tennysonian ; she forsees instinctively what

Tithonus was to learn by the bitterness of experience, that human ambition and human fate are guerdon enough for humanity, and that the gifts of the gods are only too often a sheer hindrance to mortal progress. The same Tennysonian doctrine is at the back of "Christ in Hades." The Saviour of the World visits the souls in prison, and His tender pity yearns to set them free. But in the very moment when He is about to raise His hand and liberate them from bondage, He remembers that the time is not yet, that all things must await the inevitable process of destiny, and that to anticipate the fate of man would be to run counter to the will of God. There was nothing new or startling in the philosophy of the situations, but they were none the less situations of eager dramatic effect, and the ardent imagination of the poet invested them with a splendid riot of imagery and illustration.

Here, it seemed, was a poet who was also a man, intensely and vividly alive, responding eagerly to the pagan call of passion, flooding the world of spirit with images from the world of sense, and ennobling the pleasures of sense with the dignity of a high spiritual descent. Apollo's call to the woman he woos has nothing of the god about it: he promises her immortality, but it is an immortality of the sense alone.

O brief and breathing creature, wilt thou cease
Once having been? Thy doom doth make thee rich,
And the low grave doth make thee exquisite.
But if thou'lt live with me, then will I kiss
Warm immortality into thy lips;
And I will carry thee above the world,
To share my ecstasy of flinging beams,

And scattering without intermission joy.
And thou shalt know that first leap of the sea
Toward me; the grateful upward look of earth,
Emerging roseate from her bath of dew,—
We two in heaven dancing,—Babylon
Shall flash and murmur, and cry from under us,
And Nineveh catch fire, and at our feet
Be hurled with her inhabitants, and all
Adoring Asia kindle and hugely bloom;—
We two in heaven running,—continents
Shall lighten, ocean unto ocean flash,
And rapidly laugh till all this world is warm.

It is not difficult to understand why such poetry took the public fancy by storm, especially in an hour when a new impulse was urgently demanded of the poet. The world was tired for the moment of the classic tradition, of the marble dignity of elaborate workmanship, and of what was beginning to be suspected as a cold formalism. It wanted warmth and colour, which it found in this opulent and effervescing imagination. Here was dramatic dialogue which seemed to promise new life to the poetry of drama, and a new opportunity to the stage. So the theatrical managers cast their net over Stephen Phillips, and gave him the great chance, which was also to be the peril of his genius.

III

Fortunate as Phillips was in the hour of his first publication, he was even more fortunate in his first appearance as a dramatist. The great Victorians had failed upon the stage, and any man who could produce an actable poetic drama had little contemporary rivalry to contend against.

It is true that there are passages of dramatic insight in " Harold " and " Becket " more subtle and sincere than anything that Stephen Phillips ever wrote for the stage ; true also that the last act of " Strafford " contains a culminating series of dramatic moments fuller of surprise and poignancy than even the last act of " Paolo and Francesca." But neither Tennyson nor Browning had any stage-craft ; while Phillips had been bred upon the boards. What he had learnt there served him at the beginning in excellent stead. It was, to be sure, only the scaffolding of the dramatist's art, and it resembled the poet's own acting in stopping short at the machinery of the business. It had no true grasp of character, no moment of instinctive interpretation. But few dramatists have understood better how a theatrical effect will tell upon the stage, or what is the sort of dialogue that will " speak well," and penetrate across the footlights. " Paolo and Francesca " is simply full of clever stage-construction. The first appearance of the hero, silent among the talkers, owes its stage-craft, no doubt, to the tradition of " Hamlet," but it is none the less masterly. The same effect is repeated in " Herod." The protagonist, for whose first words all the house is eagerly waiting, is kept silent until the stage is cleared. An air of tip-toe expectancy is thus aroused—the very mood the dramatist needs most to evoke. It is a trick, but it never fails.

So, too, the clever contrasts between the coarse jesting of the soldiers and the intense but repressed passion of the love-scenes ; or between Francesca's native purity, on the one hand, yielding only to the necessity of an overwhelming appeal, and on the other the heartless philandering of the lecherous little Nita; or again between the rush of emotions when the murder of the lovers is discovered, and the terrible, tragic quiet of the finish—all these dramatic resources showed the hand of experience and went straight to the heart of the public. Nor was this first play, so full of fervour and romance, by any means a thing of paint and stucco alone. In "Paolo and Francesca" the poet touched with his first attempt at a stage-play his highest poetic and imaginative level. There may not be much character-drawing among the persons of the play, the motive may be elementary and plain, the tragic element itself may lean towards sentiment. Even the final lines, so highly eulogised, may have their echo in Elizabethan drama:

> She takes away my strength.
> I did not know the dead could have such hair.
> Hide them. They look like children fast asleep.

The fancy that prompted the phrase can hardly have forgotten Webster's close-knit and terrible line:

> Cover her face. My eyes dazzle. She died young.

and the Elizabethan has the advantage of an unsurpassably tragic brevity. But when criticism has said all it can, it remains indisputable that "Paolo and Francesca" is simply alive with beauty and with beautiful lines:

> PAO.: Remember how when first we met we stood
> Stung with immortal recollections.
> O face immured beside a fairy sea,
> That leaned down at dead midnight to be kissed!

O beauty folded up in forests old !
Thou wast the lovely quest of Arthur's knights ——
FRANC. : Thy armour glimmered in a gloom of green.
PAO. : Did I not sing to thee in Babylon ?
FRANC. : Or did we set a sail in Carthage bay ?
PAO : Were thine eyes strange ?
FRANC. : Did I not know thy voice ?
All ghostly grew the sun, unreal the air
Then when we kissed.
PAO. : And in that kiss our souls
Together flashed, and now they are one flame,
Which nothing can put out, nothing divide.
FRANC. : Kiss me again ! I smile at what may chance.
PAO. : Again, and yet again ! and here and here.
Let me with kisses burn this body away,
That our two souls may dart together free.

Surely no love lyric ever exceeded the intensity of this duologue, and the beauty of the language is as deep and languorous as the moonlit atmosphere it fills.

It is sad to reflect that such a triumph was not to be repeated, but there can be little question that Stephen Phillips's first play was also his best. The simple directness of the tragedy, the keen economy of effect, the nobility of the dialogue, and the lyric variety of the blank verse, raised hopes that flowered immediately into acclamation. " Here," cried the critics with almost disconcerting unanimity, " here is a poet who is destined to revive the poetic glories of the English stage." Poetry and drama had met together once more ; the fustian of Sheridan Knowles and the hot-house exoticism of Bulwer Lytton were swept away at last ! A new era was dawning for dramatic literature ; the future was full of beaconing light. Well, the expectation was not unreasonable: why was it destined to be disappointed?

IV

The little pitted speck in garnered fruit is often disregarded until it is too late; and, as it happens, there was a perilous little passage towards the end of "Paolo" which might have caused the sensitive critic apprehension:

O God, Thou seest us Thy creatures bound
Together by that law which holds the stars
In palpitating cosmic passion bright;
By which the very sun enthrals the earth,
And all the waves of the world faint to the moon.
Even by such attraction we two rush
Together through the everlasting years.
Us, then, whose only pain can be to part,
How wilt Thou punish? For what ecstasy
Together to be blown about the globe!
What rapture in perpetual fire to burn
Together!—where we are is endless fire.
There centuries shall in a moment pass,
And all the cycles in one hour elapse!
Still, still together, even when faints Thy sun,
And past our souls Thy stars like ashes fall,
How wilt Thou punish us who cannot part?

Fine, fiery lines these, and not perhaps inapplicable to their context; but perilously near, even so, to the border-line of hyperbole:

In palpitating cosmic passion bright.

It is a feverish phrase, overloaded, and all but grotesque. A little more indulgence in such exaggeration, and the decay of dignity and balance might well ensue.

Now, it is an often-repeated experience that a poet's vices are his favourite children. The purple passage is only too frequently the primrose path to the everlasting bonfire. And the worst thing that could possibly have happened to Stephen Phillips was that his next theme after "Paolo and Francesca" should be one that in its very nature fostered and fomented this passion for over-decoration and excess. Nevertheless, the evil fairy brought the fatal gift. The drama of Herod in the days of his decadence, his mind distraught with dreams of mad ambition, his heart broken by the thwarting of passionate desire, his imperial power shattered by a cataleptic seizure—this was the very theme of themes to inflame the poet's imagery to fever-point. It attacked him with all the meretricious splendour of the jewelled East. Like his own hero, he might have exclaimed in ecstasy :

> The cymbals, and the roarings, and the roses !
> I seemed to drink bright wine, and run on flames.

In those days of felicitation Stephen Phillips was often compared with Marlowe, and the likeness was by no means superficial. He had much of Marlowe's boisterous virility, much, too, of his comprehensive imagination. But he had also the dangerous capacity for turgid rhetoric which eventually led the author of "Tamburlane" into a desert land of verbiage. Open Marlowe almost where you will, you will find passages that suggest the later decorations of "Herod," "Ulysses," "Nero," and the rest :

> A wound is nothing, be it ne'er so deep ;
> Blood is the god of War's rich livery.

Now look I like a soldier, and this wound
As great a grace and majesty to me,
As if a chair of gold enamelled,
Enchas'd with diamonds, sapphires, rubies,
And fairest pearl of wealthy India,
Were mounted here under a canopy.

The fault of such imagery is not so much that it is over-fanciful as that it is violent, and when once violence invades poetry, the author's critical balance begins to fall :

" And I will think," we can conceive our poet saying
with his hero, " in gold and dream in silver,
Imagine in marble and in bronze conceive,
Till it shall dazzle pilgrim nations
And stammering tribes from undiscovered lands,
Allure the living God out of the bliss,
And all the streaming seraphim from heaven."

In such a quest, unfortunately, the universe itself is soon exhausted. The poet looks at life through Gargantua's spy-glass, and everything natural and unnatural is magnified unto a dream of Brobdingnag. Potentates wear a province on their finger ; beauty requires the Mediterranean for a mirror ; her hair falls like a cataract over the limits of the world ; nothing but a universe in flames will suffice for a mother's funeral pyre. The sphere of the poet's imagination grows like a nightmare, writhing with lurid and fantastic shapes.

He makes a compact with the elements.
And here his agents are the very winds,
The waves his servants, and the night his friend.

The fervid imagery of Stephen Phillips indeed grew and grew in vehemence, until it became one coruscating, blinding glitter of stars, waves, cataracts, meteors, and cataclysms. Everything was vast and magnificent:

> Magnificent in livery of ruin . . .
> Even magnificence of flattering . . .
> And the magnificence of idleness . . .
> Like a rose magnificently burning . . .
> A bleak magnificence of endless hope. . . .

There are some dozens more of "Magnificents" of equal scope; and their perpetual recurrence marks the poet's fall. He has ceased to take the trouble to think, and is content with the biggest, showiest word that stands ready to his purpose. But drama cannot be contrived of purple patches alone, without character or action; and the spirit of drama reluctantly but firmly deserted Stephen Phillips from the moment when he was persuaded to mistake violence for power. For a little while his inherent sense of beauty sustained him. There are noble passages in "Herod," and fine lines (though not many) in "Nero." But his construction weakened; he was content to repeat devices, such as the incident of a prophecy threatening the hero, again and again, and, as he indulged his besetting passion for rhetoric, for large words and larger symbols, for comets and roses, flames, serpents, hunger, thirst, and desolation, the shy muse crept further and further from his ear, until at last there was little left of the lyric music of his early days save sound and fury, doing their best to masquerade as power, but only too often fading away in echo, signifying nothing.

V

There is little temptation to dwell upon the decline of talent; good will may be better employed in suggesting an explanation and an excuse. Almost certainly, then, it may be affirmed that it was the theatrical element in Stephen Phillips's work and the theatrical fashion in which he came to regard life, combined with an almost stolid lack of humour, that finally drowned out the promise of his youth. He had never possessed much sense of character, nor any considerable insight into motive. But his poetic vitality would have had the strength to counterbalance these defects, if he himself had been strong enough to resist the confusion between violence and power. His opportunity was generous. He arrived at the right moment, secured the public ear at once, was backed by the approbation of the best judgment that his time could boast; almost everything seemed possible to him. But either his head was turned, or he had no wise counsellor. His tricks grew upon him; he ceased to try to break himself of them; some of his later work even suggests that he ceased altogether to take pains. It is a grey conclusion, but there still remains enough fine work to his name to protect his memory with the next generation. It must be reckoned as a misfortune for his fame that he accomplished almost nothing as a lyrist, since there is nothing like lyrical poetry to keep a name alive. The multiplication of anthologies secures it currency; but in "The Oxford Book of Victorian Verse" Stephen Phillips is represented by no more than one short, and not very characteristic, poem of eight lines. Nevertheless, he will not be forgotten.

The pageant and progress of poetry has often been likened to the Greek torch race, which was ridden by horsemen in relays, each rider carrying on the torch for his appointed stage of the course, and then tossing it, alive and flaming, to his successor. In such a contest, "where is nor first nor last," there are many competitors, upon whose achievements the final triumph depends; yet only one covers the concluding stage and passes the goal. The plaudits of the crowd are his; he is the representative of his comrades; but many half-forgotten efforts have gone to land him in the place of pride. The simile is a sound one. It still remains for the future to reveal the great poetic dramatist of our own time, who shall raise the stage to the glory and national honour which it enjoyed among the Elizabethans. We once thought we had found the man in Stephen Phillips; but fortune, turning her wheel in the very hour of fulfilment, willed otherwise. Still, in the great relay race of his poetic generation, Stephen Phillips played no mean nor negligible part. Like the creatures of his own poetry, the torch that he handed on was one of brief but splendid brilliancy. It flamed to the heaven like fiery hair, blown in the wind, and the flakes that fell from it were bright with all the jewels of the Orient. It will glow forth again, beyond doubt, in the hand of another, brighter for his high service, and forgetful of its period of eclipse.

LIONEL JOHNSON

A THING is no sooner out of fashion than it begins to appear antique ; and the literary movements of the last decade of the nineteenth century are already discounted as a curiosity by the rising generation. The attitude is natural enough ; and yet, if the truth be realised, the despised 'nineties were actually the seed-time of the most characteristic literary harvest of to-day. The apostolic succession of literature is indeed always developing new phases. Without Mr. Kipling there would have been no Mr. Masefield ; and it is undoubtedly to the faded audacities of Mr. Arthur Symons and Mr. Richard Le Gallienne that we owe the more strenuous frankness of Mr. Gilbert Cannan and Rupert Brooke. For every movement that breaks with tradition opens up the activity of the future ; and there was never a time more secretly alive with revolution than that apparently weary period which veiled its fire under the now almost forgotten label " fin du siècle." The century, for sure, was ending, and its death seemed to justify a certain atmosphere of resigned boredom. We were ourselves, in one sense, the flotsam of a passing age. But a new century was also within hail, and the promise which it held out of vigorous intellectual changes could scarcely be disregarded, even by the decadent. And so it came about that in the early 'nineties a restless stirring of literary and spiritual interest swept across the country; and not only from Oxford and Cambridge, but even more insistently from Manchester, Liverpool, Newcastle, and other clanging cities hitherto unassociated with the gentle trouble of the Muse, young men came flocking up to London in the hope of earning a livelihood with a feverish pen ; or at any rate upheld by the fiery conviction that they had a great deal to say to which the world would have perforce to find time and patience to listen. Out of these alarums and incursions arose The Rhymers' Club and "The Yellow Book"; and the literary historian of the future will find himself obliged to recognise, although he may do so with astonishment, the variety of influence and the sheer generative force which has since sprung from such small beginnings.

The Rhymers' Club, however mild its ambitions may appear to-day, was the outcome of a genuinely sincere and spiritual aspiration. A little company of young poets, all of measured means and immeasurable imagination, met from time to time round the table of a City tavern, and read aloud their latest verses. The idea was born, no doubt, in Paris, but it soon took root between London stones. Practically all the considerable young verse-writers of the day were attracted to the circle, and they discovered golden hopes blossoming in the lamplight. The great gods of the Victorian Era were falling away, one by one. Matthew Arnold and Robert Browning had left no immediate successors ; Tennyson, a majestic recluse in his sheltered island home, must soon lay down the laurel he had worn with such lustre for over forty years. The future of poetry seemed to lie at the feet of the young men, and to justify their existence they must clearly break with tradition and breathe a new spirit into the British muse. The monumental example of Tennyson, so long accepted as the contemporary standard of taste and workmanship, must be superseded. Poetry was to come down from her marble and rose-garlanded temple on the heights, and to take her place in the crowd that bustled along the Strand and Piccadilly, colliding umbrellas in the rain. Was not Poetry Life, and Life Poetry ? Let humanity be more honest, alike with regard to its passions and its struggles. There was nothing to be ashamed about in natural impulse ; the privilege of art is to glorify the emotions. Let us all tell the truth about ourselves ; it will be vastly interesting. And so the Rhymers' Club began to take the world into its confidence ; and amid all the vehement poetic protestation that kept the fire glowing at the Cheshire Cheese, it is strange to reflect upon the vision of Lionel Johnson—seated perhaps in the very corner immortalised by his glorious namesake and antithesis—pale, silent, ascetic, with eyes that faced perpetually to their proper front, and stared in unsatisfied curiosity into the secret places of life and literature. If in that London tavern he looked the least as he looked, when I first saw him in New College Hall, he must have been the fairy changeling indeed, at odds with its world, in that hopeful, enthusiastic, and rebellious crowd.

II

In dealing with personal matters one can only report the things which one has seen and heard personally; and I hope to be absolved from the accusation of egotism if I attempt in a few sentences to speak of Lionel Johnson as I knew him in those early Oxford days. I was entering upon my second year when he came up from Winchester to New College in the October of 1886; and those of us who had just shaken ourselves free of the humble status of "freshers" felt naturally curious concerning the men who were about to take our place. We looked down the freshmen's tables with avidity, and it must have been one of the first nights of term on which I first saw Lionel Johnson in his place in Hall, for his was an appearance to make an immediate impression upon the observer. Both in figure and in demeanour he was singularly unlike the ordinary public school product. He sat back against the dark oak-panelling, awaiting the inevitable "Prince of Wales's cutlets," with his arms folded across his breast, and his gaze fixed upon the opposite wall. His amazing youthfulness arrested the imagination; he looked more like the head boy of a Preparatory School than the Oxford scholar which his voluminous robe proclaimed him. He affected, all through his Oxford days, a double-breasted coat, with wide lappels, which, with his big-sleeved flowing gown, gave him the appearance of being absolutely enveloped in his clothes; he spoke sparingly, and rarely looked at his neighbour when he did speak. Inquiry revealed at once that he was a person of unusual acquirements. He had already had articles accepted in the magazines, which to a tyro of shy ambition and no present success seemed an achievement worthy of the gods. He was reputed to write Latin verse as easily as English, and to read Plato and Aeschylus for pleasure. I know not how much of this fame was actually deserved, but it gained currency like wildfire : as also did other curious reports of later activity. Thus it was whispered that Johnson was the catechumen of strange religious rites which he celebrated in his rooms facing Holywell, and that, finding night and perambulation the only sure provocatives of thought, he was in the habit of letting himself out of College in the small hours, to the imminent peril of his University career, and of roaming Port Meadow and the Iffley road in solitary communion with the immortals. No doubt, we were most of us confirmed Philistines in those days, and Convention was the mainspring of our lives. But Johnson, at any rate, made no compromise with the usual 'Varsity convention. Looking back upon the many figures that crowd the recollection of old college "rags," I am unable to recall him as taking part in any of them. Perhaps he was there upon that glorious May night, when New College went Head of the River, and we all assembled in the front quadrangle and cheered outside the Warden's lodgings, till the venerable old man appeared at his window over the lodge, with a background of ladies and young Dons, and made a speech, in his high quavering voice, which began : "Gentlemen, I have seen what no Warden of New College has ever seen before." There were several junior members of the College, lying on the grass in ecstasies not altogether dissociated from the flow of champagne which had just celebrated the occasion, and there were momentary apprehensions that the Warden was seeing more than he was intended to see. But if Johnson was there he was not among the conspicuous ; nor can I recall him around the bonfire afterwards, when sundry gay spirits, now reverend rectors of the Anglican faith, let off Roman candles in the faces of their best friends with a nonchalance that was worthy of the fiery ordeals of the Martyrs of St. Giles.

It may very well be true, of course, that in his own way Johnson took pleasure in all these uproarious joys, and that he knew and cared something for the fine defeat of Cambridge at Lord's at the end of his first year, and for the brilliant achievements of Christopherson in the autumnal Parks. But for the most part it is more probable that such echoes troubled him but little. He was essentially a bookman, and to many of us, perhaps, the first natural bookman that we had ever been privileged to meet. Certainly he was the first man of my own age that I had encountered who picked his words, and talked with any sense of form. We were accustomed, of course, in our schoolmasters and in the " dons " to a certain precision of phrase, which seemed the monopoly of the pedagogue. But it was quite another thing that a youth of our own standing, with the features of a maiden of seventeen, should with " crystal lips Athenian speech recall," and that without any air of deliberate preciosity, but simply, as it were, from natural choice of the inevitable phrase. When Johnson had finished with " Mods," and started reading for his final schools, he spoke with impatient contempt of the " vile Greats' Jargon," which was the common medium for the philosophy essays of that generation. Some of us, who had accepted the habit without question, as part of the business required by the examiners, were a little taken aback by this presumptuous criticism. But now, in our grey years, we all know that he was right. " The vile Greats' Jargon " was no language for the man who had grown, from his youth up, under the mellow influence of Pater and of Newman.

There are many ways in which Oxford plays upon the soul of man ; and, when we look back upon those golden opportunities after many days, all but the most self-satisfied of us must be conscious of innumerable chances squandered. But that Lionel Johnson brought away from Oxford the best that she has to offer to the scholar and the poet, it is impossible to doubt even for a moment. He seems to have taken no account of her tangible rewards. The statistician will hunt for his name in vain among the prize-lists. It would not indeed be surprising to learn that Winchester was a little disappointed with his University career. But when he left Oxford he carried with him, as an abiding inspiration for life, the sweet reasonableness, the reverence for tradition, and the love of scholarship and the life of ideas, which lie at the heart of that final secret which none can utter—that unspoken password which none the less binds generation to generation of Oxford's grateful sons :

> That is the Oxford strong to charm us yet :
> Eternal in her beauty and her past.
> What, though her soul be vexed ? She can forget
> Cares of an hour : only the great things last.

Only the gracious air, only the charm,
And ancient might of true humanities:
These, nor assault of man, nor time, can harm;
Not these, nor Oxford with her memories.

Nor were the memories confined to books and to intellectual satisfactions. Johnson made many friends at Oxford, and he had a graceful habit of ascribing his different poems to the friends with whom they seemed most closely associated in his mind. Readers of the collected edition of his work, will recognise that half the Wykehamists of Johnson's generation are celebrated in this friendly fashion. Campbell Dodgson, H. B. Irving, Edward St. Leger, Hugh Orange, Arthur Galton, Nowell Smith, Basil Williams, Claud Schuster, William Busby, Arthur Clutton-Brock—it is a company of congenial spirits for whom any man might well be grateful. But it is essentially a company of the intellectuals, and probably each of them would admit that what chiefly drew their sympathies together was interest in the same authors, and enthusiasm for the same literary and poetic ideals. For a passion for intellect and an almost religious loyalty to tradition were Oxford's gifts to Lionel Johnson; and it was with these for beaconing guides that he came up to London in 1890, and, without devoting himself to any recognised profession or calling, assumed the consolatory burden of the literary life.

III

These Oxford reminiscences are, I fear, all too trivial, but they will be seen in their way to bear a direct relation to the poetry of Lionel Johnson, poetry which was in a very special sense the sincere and deep expression of his spiritual life. For Johnson's mind and taste were less affected by contact with the world of action than any man's I ever met. Winchester laid the foundation of his temperament, Oxford built upon it, and London may perhaps have completed the building; but it was the classical inspiration, bred of the Wykehamist cast of thought, which was responsible for every idea and every form of expression that he was to develop later on. Winchester was to Johnson " more than mother."

> There was beauty, there was grace,
> Each place was an holy place:
> There the kindly fates allowed
> Me too room; and made me proud,
> Prouder name I have not wist!
> With the name of Wykehamist.

And if we ask what was the true source of this pride, and what its refreshing grace, we shall find in it exactly the same elements as moved and dignified his later loyalty to Oxford. Winchester was the home of high literary associations, the Mother of great names.

> Thee, that lord of splendid lore,
> Orient from old Hellas' shore,
> Grocyn, had to mother: thee,
> Monumental majesty
> Of most high philosophy
> Honours, in thy wizard Browne:
> Tender Otway's dear renown,
> Mover of a perfect pity,
> Victim of the iron city,
> Thine to cherish is: and thee,
> Laureate of Liberty.

Tradition and Change

The young poet wandered by the Water Meads in the June twilight, or watched the glimpses of the moon in Chamber Court, dreaming not of some beckoning future that awaited his own effort, but always of the past, always of the spiritual company of the elect to which books, and familiarity with their authors, have the power of admitting the receptive soul. Even a country tramp, over the open down, in the teeth of the wind, brought him the same meditative message.

Old, rain-washed, red-roofed streets,
Fresh with the soft South-west :
Where dreaming memory meets
Brave men long since at rest.

And at Oxford inevitably his imagination was filled full of the pageantry of the years.

City of weathered cloister and worn court ;
Gray city of strong towers and clustering spires :
Where art's fresh loveliness would first resort ;
Where lingering art kindled her latest fires.

Where on all hands, wondrous with ancient grace,
Grace touched with age, rise works of goodliest men:
Next Wykeham's art obtain their splendid place
The zeal of Inigo, the strength of Wren.

Where at each coign of every antique street,
A memory hath taken root in stone :
There, Raleigh shone ; there, toiled Franciscan feet;
There, Johnson flinched not, but endured, alone.

There, Shelley dreamed his white Platonic dreams ;
There, classic Landor throve on Roman thought ;
There, Addison pursued his quiet themes ;
There, smiled Erasmus, and there, Colet taught.

Lionel Johnson

Wherever Johnson found himself, his first thought was for the associations of the place, its traditions, legends, and the heroic forms that haunted its avenues ; the spirit of the classic education had so permeated his life that he lived always in the world of dreams rather than in the world of actualities.

Dreaming still, then, his fancy perpetually fortified by high examples, he came up to London, and embarked upon the literary life. He had made good friends at Oxford—among them in particular Walter Pater, who exercised more influence upon his character than any man of his own time—and he soon found plenty of work. His early criticisms in the " Anti-Jacobin " were noticed at once : their mature manner and the rich allusiveness of their style were bound to attract attention. He also did signed work in the " Academy," then, under the editorship of Mr. J. S. Cotton, a splendid training ground for young critics ; and, above all, he joined the Rhymers' Club, and found in their periodical meetings an incentive (the very thing he most needed) to keep his hand in with poetry no less than prose. Apparently his fellow rhymers did not regard his contributions to their symposia very seriously ; for Mr. Ezra Pound, in the introduction to the Collected Poems, remarks that Johnson's friends, " with the sole exception of Mr. Yeats, seem to regard him as a prose-writer who had inadvertently strayed into verse." Now, that is a very interesting judgment, as reflecting the impression which Johnson made upon this little company of contemporary revolutionists. It illustrates vividly the isolation of his literary life. The surrounding movement was essentially one of emancipation. There were Celtic poets in the coterie, and Cymric poets, and poets of the London streets, and celebrants of the naked passions ; but among all of them the dominant impulse was a determination to stir poetry out of the rut into which the crowd of Tennysonian euphuists had driven it. The rapt visionary on the one hand, and the eager realist upon the other, were at least united in this. The dust of ages had to be beaten out of the bookshelves : a new sincerity was to make all things plain : tradition must be broken with, and the contemporary world interpreted in the light of some burning new idea.

Lionel Johnson, on the contrary, felt no need for new ideas : for him " the old was still the true." Turning back to the still honoured classics, he was content to draw from them all the inspiration that he needed for his contemplative and contented life :

Fain to know golden things, fain to grow wise,
Fain to achieve the secret of fair souls :
His thought, scarce other lore need solemnise,
Whom Virgil calms, whom Sophocles controls.

Whose conscience Aeschylus, a warrior voice,
Enchaunted hath with majesties of doom :
Whose melancholy mood can best rejoice,
When Horace sings, and roses bower the tomb :

Who, following Cæsar unto death, discerns
What bitter cause was Rome's, to mourn that day :
With austere Tacitus for master, learns
The look of empire in its proud decay :

Whom dread Lucretius of the mighty line
Hath awed, but not borne down: who loves the flame
That leapt within Catullus the divine,
His glory, and his beauty, and his shame.

And so to Plato, Thucydides, Propertius, and Pliny. Whatever the mood, the classic mould can justify it: the classic utterance is a vindication of itself.

IV

Johnson, then, comes to be considered as a poet standing somewhat aloof from the spirit of his generation, filling the function which Bagehot would have described as that of "a check or balance" upon the contemporary movement, which was all for expressing emotion in the red-hot instant of its experience. It was, no doubt, this critical and interpretative attitude, in the midst of half-realised creation, that caused his friends to regard Johnson as a "prose-writer who had strayed inadvertently into poetry." This detached, analytic loyalty to the past, scrupulously searching for the exact word, and always more interested in ideas than in men, was out of tune with the time, and may even have appeared retrograde and retarding. And indeed it would be difficult to combat the criticism that Johnson was always more interested in things than in people, in tradition than in hope, in achievement than in expectation. Nevertheless the influence of the past, critically appreciated, is a shining guide for the present, and never without its motive power upon the future.

The discerning critic indeed is never likely to pass by the name of Johnson, when he comes to recount the poetic honours of the nineteenth century. There is very little emotion in his work; he seldom sets the pulse racing or the cheek aglow ; his key is perpetually in a minor. Loving tradition as he did, it was natural that, when he gave serious thought to religion, he should have finally anchored himself in the sheltered harbour of the Roman Church ; but even his Catholicism was a faith of comfortable repose. The ideas which it embodied were ideas that appealed to the scholar's intellect ; and, when his criticism was here confronted with history, he would be content to forget the fanatical horrors of the Inquisition while meditating upon the saintly humanity of St. Francis of Assisi or the fair Athenian eloquence of Cardinal Newman. There were many Catholic poets of our day, but Johnson owes little to any of them. In Coventry Patmore Catholicism expanded into the mellow sunlight of universal and all-pervading love ; in Francis Thompson it was a quest of fierce intensity over a hillside of sand and thorns ; for Ernest Dowson it appeared like some tranquil vision in the hour of the Angelus, a rose-red revelation of the Grail, " crowning memorially the last of all our days." To Johnson it was none of these things so much as an ordered habit of the mind, a discipline of the imagination, a seemly chain of tradition binding every generation with gold chains about the feet of God. Nor was it for a moment to be detached from Pagan associations, waging war with passions which it was destined to supersede or to rectify. Among the Umbrian hills it is natural to recall to memory St. Francis among his birds ; but his figure need not obliterate the earlier glories of Propertius, or make us ashamed of taking pleasure in the jovial compensations of life. It is simply a matter of mood : the Pagan can claim his hour, and the ascetic his no less.

We to thy shade, with song and wine,
Libation make, Propertius !
While suns or stars of summer shine,
Thy passionate music thrills through us :
Hail to thee, hail ! We crown thee, thus.

But when our hearts are chill and faint,
Pierced with true sorrow piteous :
Francis ! our brother and God's Saint,
We worship thee, we hail thee, thus :
Praying, *Sweet Francis ! pray for us.*

O city on the Umbrian hills :
Assisi, mother of such sons !
What glory of remembrance fills
Thine heart, whereof the legend runs :
These are among my vanished ones.

The Celtic element in his poetry, again, of which a great deal has been made, seems to me to share with his Catholicism the quality of being, above all things, a literary and artistic interest. He has none of the true Celtic glamour of Mr. W. B. Yeats, the poetic fervour of the mystic rose ; a Celtic suggestion charms him mainly because it is such stuff as poems are made of, and imbued with the tradition of the past.

And therefore, on a night of heavenly fires ;
And therefore, on a windy hour of noon ;
Our soul, like nature's eager soul, aspires,
Finding all thunders and all winds our friends :
And like the moving sea, love we the moon ;

And life in us the way of nature wends,
Ardent as nature's own, that never tires.
Born of wild land, children of mountains, we
Fear neither ruining earth, nor stormy sea :
Even as men told in Athens, of our sires :
And as it shall be, till the old world ends.

Even the woes of Ireland are assuaged by the memory of her heroic history, and the pride of romance which she hands down to her children's children.

And yet great spirits ride thy winds : thy ways
Are haunted and enchaunted evermore.
Thy children hear the voices of old days
In music of the sea upon thy shore,
In falling of the waters from thine hills,
  In whispers of thy trees :
A glory from the things eternal fills
Their eyes, and at high noon thy people sees
Visions, and wonderful is all the air.
  So upon earth they share
Eternity : they learn it at thy knees.

"They learn it at thy knees." There in a phrase is the secret of all Lionel Johnson's inspiration : he remained through life the eager scholar, bending his soul to discipline, lowering his ear to catch the echoes of the past, drenching his fancy in the fountain of ideas, always submissive, but submissive only to the best. The heroes of his imagination, Plato, Julian, Lucretius, St. Columba, King Charles, Matthew Arnold, Cardinal Newman, Parnell, were all idealists who came through suffering into consolation; all dreamers who caught some glimpse of the vision of life, and endured in that light through dark and troublous days. And always that light was the light of the living idea, now true, now only half true, but never vain nor disconsolate. In the company of such dreamers, and in the sharing of their vision, Lionel Johnson found an abiding and infallible philosophy.

V

A life so fortified, so amply equipped with the riches of the spirit, might reasonably have been expected to prolong itself into a ripe and beneficent maturity. But, as everyone knows, Lionel Johnson died a young man : and most people who knew him know the reason. It remains one of the tragic paradoxes of one's memory that a man so fully attuned to discipline, so careful in the punctilious ordering of his art, so apparently self-contained and self-restrained, should nevertheless have proved incapable of ordering his own life, or of inspiring it with that fine austerity which ennobled all his workmanship. Most lives, it is true, carry their own secret, and there are many horse-hair shirts beneath the purple and fine linen of the public wear. But the premature decay of Johnson's delicate frame, and the early scattering of all his golden dreams, is certainly one of the greyest tragedies of the literary life in our generation. The Dark Angel that pursued him even into the secret places of prayer and penance was apparently too powerful to be overcome. He fought it in the Holy Name, but its baleful breath infected every brave activity of his life.

Through thee, the gracious Muses turn
To Furies, O mine Enemy!
And all the things of beauty burn
With flames of evil ecstasy.

Because of thee, the land of dreams
Becomes a gathering place of fears:
Until tormental slumber seems
One vehemence of useless tears.

When sunlight glows upon the flowers,
Or ripples down the dancing sea:
Thou, with thy troop of passionate powers,
Beleaguerest, bewilderest, me.

The struggle was long sustained, but at last the bewilderment swept down in a final nightmare of oblivion, and the gentle, grave, transcendent spirit of Lionel Johnson was at peace with itself and with its vision.

I fight thee, in the Holy Name!
Yet, what thou dost, is what God saith:
Tempter! should I escape thy flame,
Thou wilt have helped my soul from Death . . .

Do what thou wilt, thou shalt not so,
Dark Angel! triumph over me;
Lonely, unto the Lone I go;
Divine, to the Divinity.

What is the solution of such an enigma? Art so orderly, vision so sedate, aspiration so benign: and yet this distracting failure to realise the full measure of the talent bestowed in trust! What is the secret? Is it, perhaps, the old recurring truth that the life of ideas is not in itself enough; that the guerdon of the dreamer is after all only partial and incomplete ; that man cannot live by art alone, nor thrive for long upon tradition and the fair phantoms of the past ? It may be that, among all the precepts of the Greek philosophers so dear to his heart, there was one which Lionel Johnson was too readily disposed to forget : the truth that man is primarily a social being, and that the only perfect life, four-square to all the winds of fortune, is the life that is lived in the crowd, and devoted to the honourable and self-sacrificing service of humanity. It may be so. Dreams are the soul's most tantalising luxury, and in the strength of them man has endured, over and over again in the history of the world, the very pangs of hell itself. But dreams, like the will-o'-the-wisp, lead sometimes into the quagmire, and then the end is desolation. And yet, never quite that, in the instance of the artist. For his work survives, a fabric to endure long after this chequered vigil of existence has faded into the shadows. And the strange, sweet visions and high ideals, which made music in Lionel Johnson's life, have left their record in English poetry, a record that will wake an echoing response, so long as noble dreams are dreamed, and the triumphing traditions of pure literature stand fast.

THE TRAGEDIES OF MR. ARTHUR SYMONS

THE moss soon grows on a literary reputation; and though it seems but a little while since the work of Mr. Arthur Symons was regarded as the last word in modernity and boldness, the youngest generation would now, no doubt, discount him as out-of-date. Nevertheless, the school which is now becoming middle-aged is protected by many precedents. Whatever may have been its shortcomings, it did at least know how to write verse; it was a school of artists and of craftsmen. To open Mr. Symons's volume of "Tragedies" after a surfeit of the neo-Georgians is like entering a stately, flowering garden after fighting one's way through a tangled thicket. The new men may have all the power and the glory of undisciplined and riotous emancipation; but the poets who came into their kingdom a quarter of a century ago worshipped their art as a religion, and filled its precincts with the atmosphere of reverent devotion. They understood at least two secrets; that strength is a very different thing from violence, and that the tenderest feeling always expresses itself in the simplest terms. Strength and simplicity are indeed the cardinal virtues of the tragic muse; and when they are united, the poet's art issues with vital and unmistakable effect.

Surely, it is rather strange that this elementary principle should be so frequently disregarded.

Literature is simply starred with its proofs. All the most pathetic passages on record are irradiated by simplicity.

Joseph is not, and Simeon is not, and ye will take Benjamin away: all these things are against me.

Could the tongue of man frame tenderer phrases or simpler?

And, father cardinal, I have heard you say
That we shall see and know our friends in heaven.
If that be true, I shall see my boy again.

Pathos and simplicity could no further go.

Here, mother, tie
My girdle for me, and bind-up this hair
In any simple knot: ay, that does well.
And yours, I see, is coming down. How often
Have we done this for one another! Now
We shall not do it any more.

Deed and word are reduced to the simplest terms; but the sense of tears in the audience is overwhelming.

It is to such high examples that Mr. Arthur Symons leads us back; and the contrast between his powerful, restrained craftmanship and the turgid, irresolute vehemence of so much modern verse might serve as an object-lesson to the experimentalist. There is nothing fluid or facile about Mr. Symons's poetry; his blank verse is full of bold varieties, bending itself to its subject, and changing in fall and tension with the speaker's mood. But it is always poetry, always haunted by the touch of beauty, and (above all things) always clear to the imagination. It may be read aloud without difficulty; which is as much as to say that it could be spoken perfectly upon the stage. And yet its simplicity is run through and through with keen, arresting ideas, as a gold thread runs through a fabric. The attention is never tortured, and is yet never lulled to rest. The spirit of drama is as much alive in the work as the spirit of poetry.

Mr. Symons calls his three plays "Tragedies"; and one who is so loyal to the best tradition would probably be content to accept the old Aristotelian definition of tragedy, which has yet to be supplanted. No critic has hitherto contrived to better that ramifying description; and even the newest tragedies are modelled on the old pattern, with the same demands for high seriousness, completeness, scope, and beauty, working through the media of pity and of terror. Yet, if the whole definition be accepted, one of Mr. Symons's tragedies must be admitted to be misnamed, while another fails on the ground of scope, and *μέγεθος οὐκ ἐχούση* must be described as a tragic fragment rather than a tragedy complete. Yet, even with this concession, every one of the plays will be found rich in poetry and dramatic power. "Cleopatra in Judæa," to take the slightest first, is not indeed tragic in any accepted sense of the term, but it is alive with drama and with character. Cleopatra is on a visit to Herod at Jerusalem, and Herod has half decided to have her killed upon her homeward journey. His lords cry out against her. She is the "deadly weed of God," who will make Israel sin; her life is forfeit. But when Cleopatra comes before the king, she has clearly set herself to charm him by the exercise of all her arts. Her subtle and suggestive phrases wind around him like a web :

I have learned love in Egypt. All I know
I have not taught even to Antony ;
And I know all things. Have I not learned love
In Egypt ? there the wise old mud of the Nile
Breeds the dark sacred lotus, and the moon
Brims up its cup with wisdom ; I have learned
The seven charms of Isis, each a charm
To draw the stars out of the sky with love ;
The seven names of Apis, each a name
To stroke the madness out of cruel beasts ;
And I have looked into the heart of death
And death has told me all things, and I know
How to make every hour of life as great,
Terrible, and delicious, as the hour
When death tells all things.

But Herod is impenetrable to her wiles ; his passion for Mariamne cannot be shaken. Then Cleopatra begins to play with Mariamne's name. Has not Mariamne trifled with Antony ? Why, Cleopatra herself has the proof ; and, if her own spell were relaxed for a moment, Antony would doubtless range to Mariamne's side, and where Antony's fancy has once alighted, his appeal to women is irresistible. In a paroxysm of fear Herod beseeches Cleopatra to return and hold her love in fee. Without knowing it, Cleopatra has saved her own life. For Herod is afraid of losing Mariamne, if once Antony's enchantress were dead. So a scene of eager dramatic tension closes with Cleopatra's triumphal conduct to the borders of Judæa, protected by the splendours of the royal guard.

Less original in fancy, but truer to the formal

definition of tragedy, is the tragic fragment "The Death of Agrippina." The theme has been freely used by English poets, but Mr. Symons gives it a characteristically individual turn. He pictures Nero as a wanton weakling, redeemed from contempt by possessing the pathetic imagination of the poet. His imagination is his torment and his curse. He is urged by Poppæa to kill his mother, and yields out of very impotence of heart. But he is no such stuff as murderers are made of, and having, like Hamlet, become harnessed to a deed too exigent for his strength, he is left, like Macbeth, haunted by the perpetual vision of his sin. Henceforth he will know no peace. Agrippina will absorb his solitude.

She'll never die, and I must always live.

But the perfection of the poet's resource is seen in the masterpiece of the book, the completely tragic and noble drama of "The Harvesters." Here Mr. Symons has at his disposal all the elements of tragedy: a theme of sufficient scope, high seriousness of purpose, completeness of scheme, and a technical command over his medium which fills the poem with passages of rare beauty and sheer power. It is to be doubted if he has ever before produced any work of equally sustained and vivid force. The plot itself is familiar enough. The scene is laid in Cornwall at the beginning of the nineteenth century. Mary Raven, a farmer's daughter, has been betrayed by her lover, Peter Corin, and is "in trouble." The father suspects the truth, and tells the girl that, if she comes to shame, he will indeed continue to give her house and home, but will never speak one word to her again. She appeals to her lover, but he puts the question by. There is plenty of time yet. But the months roll on ; and Mary is near the birth of her child, when she meets the man in the harvest-field, and makes a last entreaty to him. He declines to marry her, and she there and then strikes him down with a sickle, dead. She is taken to gaol, where her child is born and dies. They put her on trial for murder, but she is acquitted, as having been insane at the moment. She is then set free, and returns home to find her father still the silent gorgon of his hearth, and all the neighbours ashamed to exchange a word with her. All, that is, except one—a half-fey, half-inspired child, " the village innocent," who welcomes her with snatches of song, like Ophelia, and offers her the inalienable gift of a guileless companionship. So Mary takes the wanderer's way, leaving her little world to its own relentless standards.

It is a plain story, but the poet invests it with all the intensity of a life-and-death conflict of ideals. The Cornwall of a century ago is seen to be dominated by two sombre and deathly principles—a boorish brutality, and an inhuman, inflexible hatred of what is socially recognised as sin. Michael Raven, the father, is a good man according to his own standards, but they are standards built upon convention and incapable of pity. He is the slave of names and phrases. " Shall I not say," cries his daughter :

Shall I not say
Father was wrong, father has done me wrong ?
Has he not sold my happiness and his

For heavy, empty syllables that weigh
False in the balances? There's sin, a name,
Justice, a name, repentance, right and wrong,
Names; he would hold them in his hand, and stand
Like a proud, ignorant child clutching his toys,
In God's place, more inflexible than God.
Yet to himself, the idea of his soul,
He has been true, and I to my own soul.

To this unbending tyranny of the law the daughter opposes the overwhelming call of nature. In the first flood of shame, she is naturally appalled at her own backsliding; but when she returns home, the past is suddenly revealed to her in a new light, and she justifies it in a passage of tremulous and almost irresistible appeal:

Do you know, Ann, that if you think a thing
And then forget it, and you go again
To where you had the thought, you find it there,
Waiting for you. I have come back again
Where all I did, not thought, was done; and now
I find it all before me as it was,
Not as I saw it then, but as it was,
The truth of it, the truth of what I did.

And so, when she turns upon her father, she has no longer any sense of shame or of penitence left. She has obeyed her nature, and he his; but she recognises and claims her own right to spiritual freedom. His cruelty has found her a way of escape:

You are an old man sitting by the wall,
And it is you would tie me by the hand
And call it pity, and tie me by the foot
And call it justice, and you would give me bread,
And let me hate the bread, and call the bread

Kindness ; and you would let me slowly die
Of justice, pity, kindness ; and sit there
Crumbling away silently like the wall.
You are an old man, and you have done me wrong.
But I am young still, and I will work and live.

So she vanishes, with the wandering child, on the way of the wind, and the old man is left mumbling in a mist of sudden revelation :

Lord, Lord, if she were right, if she were right !

There is just that amount of hope for him. He has been touched at last by the passing spirit of human pity.

" The Harvesters " is a drama of deep beauty, unforced pathos, and strong human conflict. The touches of insight and character which dignify it are innumerable, and its broad, untrammelled outlook is wedded to a simple, direct, and sensitive gift of poetic expression. It challenges the world of affectation, and asserts, by merit of example, the impregnable virtues of craftsmanship and restraint. In a word, it conforms to the true tradition, and at the same time presents a criticism of life, which resolves itself into the perennial struggle between old and new ideals of conduct. The tragedy of parentage, as old as " Lear," returns to torture every passing generation. Its conflict is rooted in the simplest elements of human nature : it is the same, inevitable struggle of Tradition and Change once more.

JAMES ELROY FLECKER

THE untimely death of James Elroy Flecker, at no more than thirty years of age, unquestionably robbed modern poetry of one of its brightest and most hopeful spirits. Hopeful, indeed, was the essence of his record; for he had not yet fully come into his own. His talent developed slowly, widening its outlook by stealthy stages, and would probably have achieved successes far greater than any that yet stood to his name. The sense of all that may have been lost by his death increases as we turn over the pages of the collected edition* of all that he had already done. Nevertheless, what stands is much, and this definitive volume will finally fix his reputation among the most genuinely and spiritually inspired poets of his time. The editor's work has been scrupulously performed. A few "Juvenilia" are printed for the first time, to indicate the nature of the poet's development; one or two fragmentary pieces have been carefully put together into something like complete form; and the volume opens with a model introduction, biographical and critical, intimate but not effusive, from the pen of his friend, Mr. J. C. Squire. All that Mr. Squire has to tell his readers is of the first value in enabling them to appreciate the circumstances under which Flecker worked, and the ambition

* The Collected Poems of James Elroy Flecker. With an Introduction by J. C. Squire.

which stimulated him; the entire essay is a worthy tribute to a deep but discriminating admiration. Friendship could have done no better service to a friend.

Flecker was the son of a parson-schoolmaster, and was educated at Uppingham and Trinity College, Oxford. He seems to have been at his public school only a year, and to have left it for the University somewhat raw and undeveloped. He had begun to write verses with a rather dangerous facility, and much of his early work was mere imitation of Swinburne and Oscar Wilde. But in attempting translations from the classics, and in particular from Catullus and Propertius, he imbibed that sense of form which was always the mainspring of his workmanship, and many of his youthful verses show a remarkable originality in imagery and vision.

> Like a dull bee the steamer plies
>   And settles on the jutting pier;
> The barques, strange sailing butterflies,
>   Round idle headlands idly veer.

Such a figure as this comes from true, interpretative fancy; and the fragmentary "Ode to Shelley," written while he was still a boy, is full of glittering passages:

> Light and the subtler light of wizard fire,
> And winds that strike forth hope on some grand lyre,
> And spirits of blue air like April clouds,
> And all the water-company that crowds
> The river-spaces and dark open sea,
> Conspired at his creation: Liberty,
> Watching his prowess from her tower above,
> Took to her side a royal wingéd Love.

There are foreshadowings of the later Flecker here, but on the whole the work which he accomplished at Oxford did not hold out any very exceptional promise. It was not until he joined the consular service, and went to the East, that his imagination began to flower freely. Fate had then cast him into his fit inheritance, for the East was always Flecker's spiritual home. Its warmth, its colour, its air of mystery and faint allegiance to the eternities of the soul—all these wandering and wayward sources of inspiration began to work like leaven in his brain. And so by degrees he evolved his peculiarly individual and melodious system of craftsmanship.

That system may fairly be said to place him midway between the solid Victorian tradition and the perfervid egoism of the ultra-moderns. It was a system which, first and last, set its heart upon the indefatigable pursuit of beauty. It was intensely discontented with the prevailing taste. "Our poetic criticism, and our poetry," said Flecker himself, "are in chaos. . . . It is not the poet's business to save man's soul, but to make it worth saving." So he broke with every ideal of poetry which concentrated upon a message or a gospel; he would have nothing to do with the prettiness which served merely as a veil for the preacher. He wrote with the single intention of creating beauty—beauty of form, beauty of vision, beauty of suggestion, the pure natural enjoyment of the glory of the eyes and the splendours of dream.

> I was beyond the hills, and heard
> That old and fervent Goddess call,

Whose voice is like a waterfall,
And sweeter than the singing-bird.

O stubborn arms of rosy youth,
Break down your other Gods, and turn
To where her dauntless eyeballs burn,—
The silent pools of Light and Truth.

To this pursuit of beauty he devoted every sensitive impulse, polishing and recasting his well-wrought lines with a sheer passion for craftsmanship. He had indeed the modern's impulse to record the passing mood, but he despised the modern's easy satisfaction with a crude, untutored trick of phrase-making. He had learnt from the French Parnassians the imperishable value of style. " Read the works of Hérédia," he wrote, " if you would understand how conscious and perfect artistry, far from stifling inspiration, fashions it into shapes of unimaginable beauty." And with this example to fortify him, he would take a dawning idea, or even a suggested title, and let it germinate in his brain, slowly and elaborately, until it brought forth the perfect flower of language. His friend Mr. Frank Savery supplies an illuminating anecdote. They were sitting one day in an Oxford room, when Flecker suddenly announced that he was going to write a volume of poems, and to call it " The Bridge of Fire." " And I'll write a poem with that name and put it into the middle of the book, instead of the beginning. That'll be original and symbolic too." But what the poem was to be about he had no idea. Anyhow, " it was a jolly good title, and he'd easily be able to think of a poem to suit it." And so, with the words " The Bridge of Fire " burning in his brain, he went away, and let the phrase smoulder, and lighten, and blaze, until it broke out into his splendid vision of the gods, Persephone and Ra, Belus and Cybele, Isis and Allah, glimmering through the fire, with eyes alight upon their everlasting quest.

Between the pedestals of Night and Morning,
Between red death and radiant desire
With not one sound of triumph or of warning
Stands the great sentry on the Bridge of Fire.
O transient soul, thy thought with dreams adorning,
Cast down the laurel, and unstring the lyre ;
The wheels of Time are turning, turning, turning,
The slow stream channels deep and doth not tire.
    Gods on their Bridge above
    Whispering lies and love
Shall mock your passage down the sunless river
    Which, rolling all its streams,
    Shall take you, king of dreams,
  —Unthroned and unapproachable for ever—
To where the kings who dreamed of old
Whiten in habitations monumental cold.

This gathering imagination is typical of Flecker's art ; his poetry is essentially the poetry of vision, living upon glimpses of light and love, which flicker through a pilgrimage of hope. A golden light encompasses it all, a light that almost absorbs the outline. Compared with most of his contemporaries, his work might appear impersonal. As Mr. Squire observes, he was always more interested in his art than in himself. It was here that the classic and romantic instincts clashed in him. He was assailed by a riotous imagination, and yet restrained by a natural repulsion from anything like exuberant confidence or morbid introspection. He was perplexed by the riddle of existence, but held it no part of the poet's task to justify the ways of God to man. There was the golden road of imagination ahead of him, and the call of the spirit's pilgrimage was enough.

We are the Pilgrims, master ; we shall go
  Always a little further : it may be
Beyond that last blue mountain barred with snow,
  Across that angry or that glimmering sea,

White on a throne or guarded in a cave
  There lives a prophet who can understand
Why men were born : but surely we are brave,
  Who make the Golden Journey to Samarkand.

Of course it must be conceded that this ideal pursuit of beauty for its own sake, this pilgrimage of golden light, is not the whole task of poetry. It misses the aspiring philosophy of the seer ; it does not penetrate into the depths ; it does nothing to reconcile the soul of man to his destiny, or to explain the tragedy of human waste and sacrifice. For this supreme service of poetry it may be that Flecker died too soon. It may be also that the unfailing cheerfulness, which was only too sure a symptom of his fatal malady, sustained him in flights of the fancy where many who are weighed down by suffering will be incapable of following him. Certainly, he was always the poet of hope, and of high spiritual enthusiasm. And yet it seems, when we read his latest poems, as though his tardy maturity were just beginning to stretch out hands towards a light more blinding even than that of beauty. The poet's vision becomes suddenly irradiated by a compelling human force, which makes the sacrifice of individuality appear inevitable in the triumphant claim of a common humanity.

Sleep not, my country: though night is here, afar
Your children of the morning are clamorous for war:
Fire in the night, O dreams!
  Though she send you as she sent you, long ago,
  South to desert, east to ocean, west to snow,
West of these out to seas colder than the Hebrides
    I must go
Where the fleet of stars is anchored and the young
    Star-captains glow.

In a flash, as it were, it is revealed to him that the caravan of life may not after all be bound for a golden city, and that when "the old flag takes once more the unquestionable road," it may be destined to be draggled through dust and blood. Within a month of his death Flecker was putting the finishing touches to that noble appeal "The Burial in England," where the poet's soul faces the inevitable conflict with a malign force which has

  Dipped in that ice the pedantry of power,
  And toughened with wry gospels of dismay,

and his last message to his companions on the road is one of unquestioning endurance in an adventure which is stripped of all beauty, save that of stark and clear-eyed heroism.

Boys, drink the cup of warning dry. Face square
That old grim hazard, "Glory-or-the-Grave."
Not we shall trick your pleasant years away,

James Elroy Flecker

Yet is not Death the great adventure still,
And is it all loss to set ship clean anew
When heart is young and life an eagle poised ?
Choose, you're no cowards. After all, think some,
Since we are men and shrine immortal souls,
Surely for us as for these nobly dead
The Kings of England lifting up their swords
Shall gather at the gate of Paradise.

With that stirring word upon his lips, Flecker, who had always contended that poetry should eschew a moral message, paid his own tribute to the impartial conqueror. Death had been gaining upon him step by step ; but the beauty of life had still inspired him, and he now turned to greet the fate that followed him, and found an imperishable beauty in death itself. Pain had not chilled his courage nor depressed his dream. Like the knight of the poet's idyll, he faded into his vision, and the golden light that he had always loved so well was about him to the last.

THE IMAGISTS

DR. JOHNSON, surveying the achievement of English poetry from the earliest days to the close of the eighteenth century, decided that, so far as metrical skill and the resources of prosody could go, the English language was incapable of higher triumphs than those which decorated the muse of Alexander Pope. In Pope, he believed, the beauty and the dignity of the national language had attained their highest possible perfection ; in the future other things of note and vigour might be done, but nothing more exquisite, nothing more impeccably musical. That judgment might well serve as a text upon the futility of prophecy ; it is also in itself sufficient to give pause to the rash audacities of later criticism. The eighteenth century was an age which bestowed the most sensitive care upon the technicalities of the poet's art, and Dr. Johnson was its strongest and most representative voice. Yet he could see no farther ahead of him than to believe that the polished, mechanical couplets of "Th Rape of the Lock" were the last possible refinement of English prosody. Looking back upon all that poetry has achieved since then, criticism may well hesitate to dogmatise over new departures.

The newest movement in English verse, however, is one sufficiently disconcerting to readers trained upon tradition to make serious demands upon their patience and receptivity. The Imagists, it must be confessed, compose a strange and unfamiliar little company. At first they were generally dismissed as eccentrics ; but they have persevered in the face of discouragement, and have now several slender volumes of *vers libre* to their credit. Moreover, to their latest anthology* they have prefixed a temperate and sensible essay, setting forth clearly and without arrogance the principles upon which they work, and inviting, as they certainly deserve, a fair consideration in the light of their own aims and intentions. This essay is calculated to dispel a good deal of the misapprehension which the early excesses of " Imagism " inevitably encountered, by making it clear that, however far the products of the movement may fall short of its ambition, there is nothing in that ambition itself which cannot be made to take line with the natural processes and intentions of the poet's art.

The Imagists, we are told, base their poetry upon cadence rather than upon metre, and they define cadence as " the sense of perfect balance of flow and rhythm." In this they can hardly claim to be violent innovators ; the choruses of Æschylus are based upon no other principle, nor, for the matter of that, are the anapaestic splendours of Swinburne. But the Imagists extend the sphere of balance or flow outside the limit of the line or verse, so as to include the whole poem, and require the whole for its full effect. There must be the " circular swing of a balanced pendulum," which may complete itself in a verse, or may need a long " strophe " in

* "Some Imagist Poets." 1916. An Annual Anthology.

which to round off its harmony. " The circle need not always be the same size, nor need the time allowed to negotiate it be always the same. There is room for an infinite number of variations. . . . But one thing must be borne in mind : a cadenced poem is written to be read aloud ; in this way only will its rhythm be felt. Poetry is a spoken and not a written art. . . ." There is nothing very new in this : and, indeed, the *vers libristes* proceed to dissociate themselves from any claim to the novelty of revolution. " The name *vers libre*," they say, " is new ; the thing, most emphatically, is not." And they cite Milton, Dryden, Matthew Arnold, and W. E. Henley as illustrious forerunners in the employment of unrhymed and cadenced metres. These exemplars are worth more than a volume of theory. Matthew Arnold's " Philomela," we are told, " is a shining example " of what they are aiming at. And no one, they might well add, has found fault with the metrical excellence of

Eternal passion ! eternal pain !

In all these prolegomena the Imagist aim is reasonable enough ; but, unfortunately, this quotation of examples turns their weapon against their own breasts. For, knowing definitely what they are aiming at, we are the better able to judge of their success or failure. Let, then, anyone accustomed to the fall of poetry read, let us say, Arnold's " Philomela " and Henley's " Margaritæ Sorori," and then, with those cadences still lingering in his ears, read aloud (since the spoken sound is to be the test of poetry) H.D.'s. complete poem, " Sitalkas " :

Thou art come at length
More beautiful
Than any cool god
In a chamber under
Lycia's far coast,
Than any high god
Who touches us not
Here in the seeded grass.
Aye, than Argestes
Scattering the broken leaves.

Where are we to trace here "the complete swing of the pendulum," the strophe rounding thought and expression into a melodious whole? There is no melody in the poem at all, and the thought is as thin as the language. And here are two complete poems, two examples of "perfect balance of flow and rhythm" from the pen of Mr. Ezra Pound. Here is the first:

O fan of white silk,
    clear as frost on the grass-blade,
You also are laid aside.

And here is the second:

The petals fall in the fountain,
    the orange-coloured rose-leaves,
Their ochre clings to the stone.

Each of these utterances is offered as the completely cadenced expression of a completed thought. And in the face of such inarticulation it is simply an impertinence to quote the choral odes of "Samson Agonistes," as professing the same standard of metrical tone. Yet it is to these examples that the Imagists appeal as the foundation of their method.

Or take Miss Amy Lowell, endeavouring to

reproduce in words the effect of a string quartet playing a piece of music by M. Stravinsky:

> Bang! Bump! Tong!
> Petticoats,
> Stockings,
> Sabots,
> Delirium flapping its thigh-bones;
> Red, blue, yellow,
> Drunkenness steaming in colours;
> Red, yellow, blue,
> Colours and flesh weaving together,
> In and out, with the dance,
> Coarse stuffs and hot flesh weaving together,
> Pigs' cries white and tenuous,
> White and painful,
> White and—
> Bump!
> Tong!

What is produced here is the absolute negation of all form and expression, and we should like to hear M. Stravinsky's judgment upon this singular mistranslation of his work. So far as the essences of poetry are concerned, confusion could surely no farther go.

The trouble seems to be that the Imagists have not yet arrived at a proper understanding of their own principles, and are trying to write *vers libre* without a sufficiently trained and sensitive ear. By far the most successful of them, Mr. Richard Aldington, achieves his best effect in a poem unfortunately much too long for quotation, the really beautiful and haunting "Eros and Psyche," with which the Imagists' Annual for 1916 opens. Here, indeed, is unrhymed and cadenced verse employed with a true sense of rhythm and of beauty; here, also, are images and ideas in perfect consonance with the expression. And inferior only to this poem in the entire collection is Miss Amy Lowell's "Patterns," where, again, the imagery and the music merge into a strongly dramatic lyric of genuine force. But these pieces stand practically alone in their mastery of method. The rest is little but crude experimentalism.

Imagism, no doubt, is a natural reaction from the metrical fluency of the Victorians, just as French Symbolism was a revolt against the classic perfection of the Parnassians. But the French Symbolists, with whom the Imagists seek to ally themselves in their profession of faith, did, at any rate, know the business of verse-making; they were artists and artificers to the finger-tips. The Imagists, on the other hand, are in such a hurry to assert their independence that they have not taken time to prepare a new art with which to supplant the old. It is all very well to talk about the perfect swing of the poetic pendulum; but what is to be said when the cadence completes itself like this?

> Thy feet are white
> Upon the foam of the sea;
> Hold me fast, thou bright Swan,
> Lest I stumble,
> And into deep waters.

What, indeed, but that the feet of swans are not white, and do not lie upon the foam of the sea, and that, if the poet falls into the water, a swan would be the last creature to hold him fast? What, indeed, but that the entire "Nocturne" is nonsense, and that Imagism must be much more certain of its ground, before it can claim to usurp the place of a band of singers who knew at least what they meant to say, and said it with such perfection that a whole generation hung spellbound on their lips?

The future of *vers libre* is at present in the clouds. It may very well prove to be one of the principal poetic developments of the next generation, and it is already showing its capabilities in the hands of patient artists. But, like all novelties, it is in danger of being seized upon by the incompetent as a covert for sloppy and unconsidered workmanship. The Imagists have yet to establish the rules of their craft by the only true test of practice. When that is achieved, they will, no doubt, clear their community of a good many vain pretenders.

Mr. D. H. LAWRENCE

THE modern conception of poetry is so astonishingly different from the conception, for example, of the last generation before our own, that it is worth while to take stock of the situation now and again, and to try to get some clear notion of the direction in which we are drifting. Changes there must be, of course ; and the critic who withstands change for its own sake is self-condemned already. But in the realm of the arts there are certain fixed principles which have survived all the vagaries of fashion ; and work which has defied those principles has never lasted. Novelty and audacity attract their momentary public ; but novelty is soon stale, and audacity has an awkward way of petering out into impertinence. It is a good thing to overhaul our equipment from time to time, and to refer it by comparison to those irrefutable truths upon which all sincere art must be grounded.

Some such comparison seems to be particularly invited in the case of the poetry of Mr. D. H. Lawrence. It would appear that the newest school of criticism is in no sort of doubt about the quality of his performance ; he can point to a glittering consensus of eulogy from the Press ; and he has been admitted into that privileged circle of Georgian Poetry which issues crowned with the imprimatur of the Poetry Bookshop. And yet, surely, even those who are most completely dazzled by the novelty of his work must admit that Mr. Lawrence's verse is of a kind which, before the coming of the most recent impressionist movement in letters, not gods, nor men, nor booksellers have ever recognised under the name of poetry. Much controversy, of course, has raged from time immemorial around the limits of the poet's art ; and (to go no further back than our own time), since the experiments of Robert Browning were recognised at their true value, the boundaries of poetry have been perpetually enlarged. But two essentials have hitherto been required inexorably of the poet : it has been demanded of him that his work should be dominated by an idea, and that the idea should be expressed in terms of technical beauty. Without an animating idea a poem drifts away into a mist of words ; without beauty, alike of vision and of melody, the form of the expression degenerates into mere rhetoric. All the great poetry in all languages will be found to base its claim upon these two qualities : it has survived by virtue of the ideas that it expresses, and by the perfect beauty of the expression in which those ideas are embodied and translated into words.

Mr. Lawrence, on the contrary, is a typical representative of a literary movement which deliberately eschews these qualities. He is concerned not with ideas but with moods, while the object of his art is to express those moods with as much vivid actuality as he can cram into metrical form, without regard for the restraints or responsibilities of prosody or technique. If the metre will hold the bubbling mood within its cup, all well and good ; but if the mood runs over the metre's brim—never mind, let it go; the one thing needful is to keep the realism of the passionate moment intact. So you write like this, and impressionism is held justified of its effect:

Into a deep pond, an old sheep-dip,
Dark, overgrown with willows, cool, with the brook
    ebbing through so slow,
Naked on the steep, soft lip
Of the bank I stand watching my own white shadow
    quivering to and fro.

What if the gorse flowers shrivelled and kissing were
    lost?
Without the pulsing waters, where were the mari-
    golds and the songs of the brook?
If my veins and my breasts with love embossed
Withered, my insolent soul would be gone like
    flowers that the hot wind took.

And you make no trouble about a clash of discordant consonants:

Though her kiss betrays to me this, this only
Consolation, that in her lips her blood at climax clips
Two wild, dumb paws in anguish on the lonely
Fruit of my heart, ere down, rebuked, it slips.

And if a Cockney rhyme falls easily into its place, you leave that standing also:

Over the nearness of Norwood Hill, through the
    mellow veil
Of the afternoon glows to me the old romance of
    David and Dora,
With the old, sweet, soothing tears, and laughter
    that shakes the sail
Of the ship of the souls over seas where dreamed
    dreams lure the unoceaned explorer.

It was not so that they sang in the golden days, when Plancus was consul; but Plancus himself, no doubt, is out of date to-day, and the new impressionism aims rather at violent effect than at charmed and charming minstrelsy. Mr. Lawrence is only too wisely aware that his audacities will shock convention, and forestalls the criticism in a pungent quatrain:

Ah, my darling, when over the purple horizon shall loom
The shrouded mother of a new idea, men hide their faces,
Cry out, and fend her off, as she seeks her procreant groom,
Wounding themselves against her, denying her fecund embraces.

Let us, then, at any rate not hide our faces; but do our best to follow the "shrouded mother" to the secret nuptials of mood and expression. It is not always an easy path, for the poet's method (as perhaps our quotations have already suggested) is congenitally obscure and murky. Nevertheless, by degrees a certain recognisable scheme appears to emerge from the tangle of Mr. Lawrence's over-heated phrase-making, and that scheme is evidently deliberate and purposeful.

The principle of Mr. Lawrence's poetry, then (as it seems to one sincere, if somewhat uninitiated reader), is the exposition in high light of a momentary mood, preferably sensuous, expressed in glowing terms of an elaborately-wrought symbolism of the senses. As the nature-poets of the nineteenth century represented the heaven and earth as sharing in the emotions of humanity, and so set their pictures in a harmonious environment of storm and sunlight; so Mr. Lawrence, allowing his imagination freer rein, conceives the whole natural world as a passionate allegory of human desire, human satisfaction, and human satiety. This world of emotion is physical, not spiritual. The very flowers, in a riot of suggestion, tempt the lover to the gratification of his desire; the roving bee is a profligate ravisher of innocence. The earth is full of hidden imagery, and its apparent peace is tortured by secret sensuality:

You amid the bog-end's yellow incantation,
You sitting in the cowslips of the meadow above,
Me, your shadow on the bog-flame, flowery may-
    blobs,
Me full length in the cowslips, muttering you love;
You, your soul like a lady-smock, lost, evanescent,
You with your face all rich, like the sheen of a dove.

And again:

Ah, love, with your rich, warm face aglow,
What sudden expectation opens you
So wide as you watch the catkins blow
  Their dust from the birch on the blue
Lift of the pulsing wind—ah, tell me you know

Ah, surely! Ah, sure from the golden sun
A quickening, masculine gleam floats in to all
Us creatures, people and flowers undone,
  Lying open under his thrall,
As he begets the year in us. What then, would you
    shun?

The entire firmament is summoned to assist the lover in his wooing; and virgin youth is displayed as a tossing torrent of "urgent, passionate waves," where "docile, fluent arms" knot themselves " with wild strength to clasp " the imagined nymph ; where the body is all a " wild strange tyranny," and the eyes reassert themselves with difficulty in " relentless nodality." It will be conceived that this riotous symbolism can soon become uncommonly sultry ; indeed, if there is a more suggestive poem in the English language than " Snapdragon," we should be sorry to be set the task of unravelling its allegory.

Well, what are we to make of it all ? For Mr. Lawrence is clearly not a writer to be dismissed in a flash of quotation. He has caught the ear of critics who demand respect. He has an overwrought, perverted, but very powerful imagination. You may not like him, but you cannot deny that he cuts into your perception. His lack of taste may revolt you, but he hits his mark. He is not negligible, though you may confess that there are times when his fancy seems little less than disgusting. He can write, undoubtedly : but does he write poetry ? If so, it is certainly a sort of poetry that runs upon entirely different lines from all the proved traditions of the past. Technically, it is at intervals only a little less inchoate than Walt Whitman, and in expression it is invariably much more nebulous. The poet indulges his symbolism until it becomes his master ; his fecund fancy overwhelms him, like the serpents of Laocoön. He is perpetually struggling with his own wilful and contorted metaphors. Almost every verse that he writes requires to be read more than once, before its meaning takes definite shape in the mind ; and by dropping the connecting links of his thought, in a sort of post-Browningesque obliquity, he is apt to render confusion doubly confounded. Worst of all, he does outrageous violence to Nature, by dragging her beauties into a sort of guilty condonation of the excesses of his imagination ; he is not ashamed to ravish the goddess Flora in sudden spasms of a tortured imagery. What Mr. Lawrence's art stands most desperately in need of is a shower-bath of vital ideas. At present his fancy is half asleep upon a fœtid hot-bed of moods. It is a vigorous, masculine fancy, but it seems to have got into bad company, and to have been left deserted on a midden. Perhaps some vivifying, ennobling, human experience will yet help it to save its soul alive.

Mr. J. C. SQUIRE

WHEN a poet begins to sift and weed out his poetry, we see and know for ourselves that the day of his maturity is at hand. Youth is very jealous of its achievements; the last production may indeed be valued the most highly, but all are treasures to be defended against alien criticism. All are part of the poet's self; and, even when we begin to grow old, it is our self that commands our longest loyalty. The man who has learnt to hold himself at arm's length, and to test himself with the eyes of criticism, is already master of half the secrets that go to make up a well-balanced and harmonious life.

Some men, however, pass the barrier more easily than others; and when Mr. J. C. Squire emerges from his study with a selected volume containing "all that he does not wish to destroy" from the contents of four highly-popular books of verse,* it does not astonish us, so much as it might in other cases, to find that the salvage is of unnecessarily modest bulk. For the cast of Mr. Squire's mind has always been critical; his art lives and flourishes in a permanent tribunal of judgment. The whole concern of his literary activity lies in testing whatever may be presented to his imagination. He tests the methods of the masters; he tests their spiritual ideals; he tests the world that lies around him; he tests

* "Poems." First Series. By J. C. Squire.

his own attitude to that world, assiduously analyses his conception of its problems. A modern of the moderns, he can yet judge modernity in its relation to the past. His is not one of those half-fledged intellects, which imagines that art and interpretation began to exist the day before yesterday. He appreciates (no man more intimately) the claim of beauty ; but he has learnt to realize that beauty is not a thing of prettiness and favour. He has swept aside sentimentality, but he discriminates between sentimentality and sentiment. With so closely woven a net continually ready to his hand, it is not surprising that he should permit very little to survive which is tainted with the old-fashioned vices of slushiness and facility.

This " First Series " of his poems is a collection of rare quality ; but there will be some of its readers to wish it larger. Was it necessary, for example, to omit all those interpretative parodies with which Mr. Squire first took the fancy of the town ? To be sure, parody and serious poetry do not range perfectly together ; but the reader who would understand Mr. Squire's literary temperament is bound to take his parodies into consideration first of all. For they display, as no amount of comment could possibly display, his critical faculty, clearing the ground for its own creation. Mr. Squire belongs (inevitably) to that younger generation which was born tired of the technical ease and grace of its immediate predecessors. It found technical excellence brought to a point where expression was poured into a mould so elaborate that the mould had become the very condition of the thought expressed.

The manner of saying a thing, in short, counted for more than the quality of the thing said ; and all the mountain of the Muses was haunted by echoes so insidious that they threatened to suppress individuality altogether. These echoes the travesty of Mr. Squire set itself to scatter to the winds. He seizes upon a much-admired melody and tears the stuffing out of it in a moment :

Thunder in the halyards and horses leaping high,
Blake and Drake and Nelson are listenin' where
    they lie,
Four and twenty blackbirds a-bakin' in a pie—

And, in a flash, all the magic of the new sea-chanty is detected, and dissolved into the mist of an old nursery rhyme.

But Mr. Squire differs from the average iconoclast in tempering his rebellion with a faultless sense of form. He refuses to be beguiled by the outworn metrical methods of the Tennysonian and Swinburnian euphuists ; but his ear is much too sensitive to accept in exchange the flat wastes of *vers libre* and of incoherent imagism. Testing (as is his wont) the lyrical conventions which have grown stale through their own perfecting, he decides that the consequent evolution leads, out of a metre which confines and cripples the thought, into a wider and more versatile harmony which shall permit the thought to modulate and attune the metre. And his most conspicuous contribution to modern prosody lies in the variety and suppleness of his metrical effect, in which the melody sways to suit the mood, the long line growing with the crescent thought, and the thought sinking back into the short line, as the completed idea crystallizes to its close. The river of song follows the course of the river of imagination, beckoning the fancy to a realm which is neither memory nor anticipation, but something that hovers presciently between the two.

There, there, where the high waste bog-lands
And the drooping slopes and the spreading valleys,
The orchards and the cattle-sprinkled pastures
    Those travelling musics fill,
There is my lost Abana,
And there is my nameless Pharphar
That mixed with my heart when I was a boy,
    And time stood still.

And I say I will go there and die there :
But I do not go there, and sometimes
I think that the train could not carry me there,
    And it's possible, maybe,
That it's farther than Asia or Africa,
Or any voyager's harbour,
Farther, farther, beyond recall. . . .
    O even in memory !

None of the younger poets, it may safely be affirmed, has experimented so boldly, and to such rich effect, in new metrical patterns. Mr. Squire has learnt a good deal, no doubt, from Mr. Robert Bridges ; but the young poet goes further than the old in the interchange of cadences, the audacity of pause and recovery, the secure reliance upon the reader's sympathetic ear. If he were to be judged by his prosody alone, the author of "The Lily of Malud" would take undisputed rank among the most emancipating of the innovators.

But Mr. Squire is very far from being a metrist alone ; it is the matter even more than the manner of his poetry which compels attention. As his parodies once more suggest, his work is a natural reaction from the sentiment of the idyllic poets who swamped the lower levels of the Victorian Parnassus. He returns to Nature, but to the Nature of a crowded civilization rather than to the solitude of field and fell. The lodestar of life to the new generation must lie in a world of action. It is vanity to dream about the past. The present is the inevitable concern of a living man :

Never despise the things that are.
Set your teeth upon the grit.
Though your heart like a motor beat,
Hold fast this earthly star,
The whole of it, the whole of it.

But it is the star itself that must be followed, not its reflection in the swamp. The lily of Malud is indeed born in secret mud ; but, when it has once blossomed, it makes for itself a world of beauty that conceals the bed of ugliness and squalor from which it sprang.

For Beauty with her hands that beckon
  Is but the Prophet of a Higher,
A flaming and ephemeral beacon,
  A Phœnix perishing by fire.
Herself from us herself estranges,
  Herself her mighty tale doth kill,
That all things change yet nothing changes,
  That all things move yet all are still.

I cannot sink, I cannot climb,
  Now that I see my ancient dwelling,
The central orb untouched of time,
  And taste a peace all bliss excelling.

Now I have broken Beauty's wall,
  Now that my kindred world I hold,
I care not though the cities fall
  And the green earth go cold.

In this spirit the poet chooses, as his symbol of life, the plain, unideal house-roof which overlays and covers all the essential hours of love and suffering. The roof is an ugly enough object in itself; but, set on high, face to face with the heaven above, it reflects the beauty of the passing hours—the lights of dawn, the mystical shadows of twilight—and it is visited, in its secret places, by the voices of peace and love. And out of these voices emerge those strange, meditative moments when the soul, alone with itself, is aware of the hidden meaning and purpose of life. The stars above the roof open a door into eternity:

They draw the long-untraversed portal,
  Our souls slip out and tremble and expand,
The immortal feels for the immortal,
  The eternal holds the eternal by the hand.

Impalpably we are led and lifted,
  Softly we shake into the gulf of blue,
The last environing veil is rifted
  And lost horizons float into our view.

Lost lands, lone seas, lands that afar gleam
  With a miraculous beauty, faint yet clear,
Forgotten lands of night and star-gleam,
  Seas that are somewhere but that are not here.

And here the pilgrimage of man is seen to be moving in a circle; for these moments of dream bring back the past to the imagination, with a bitter conviction of our mortal change, our infidelity to old friendships, our disloyalty to ideals once cherished and adored. For man is a fugitive all his days, escaping as best he may from the wilderness of his own passions, guarding as sacred to himself the lonely secrets of his heart :

> Vanishing now who would not stay
> To the blue hills on the verge of day.
> O soft ! soft ! Music play,
>   Fading away,
>   (Fleet are his feet
>   And his heart apart)
> Fading away.

From such an evading flight, however, Thought must hale man back into the world of action. Overmuch thought corrodes the soul :

> Thought is putrefaction
> If thought is all in all !

It has been too often the fault of poetry to waste in passionate dreams ; and this poet, at any rate, would brook no spiritual servitude in a garden of lotus-flowers. Out of weakness must come strength : out of ugliness beauty. Perhaps, after all, there is neither ugliness nor beauty : but thinking makes it so.

> And though I am vague and shrink to guess
> God's everlasting purposes,
> And never save in perplext dream
> Have caught the least clear-shapen gleam
> Of the great kingdom and the throne
> In the world that lies behind our own,
> I have not lacked my certainties,
> I have not haggard moaned the skies,
> Nor waged unnecessary strife,
> Nor scorned nor undervalued life.

A warm-hearted, inspiring gospel this, and a brave spirit in which to confront the opening day! The poet here offers no braggart defiance to fate ; he consoles himself with no shadowy vision of a continuing city ; he is neither Stoic, nor Epicurean. But, " having cast much cant," and come to terms with life, he is assured that in effort, in companionship, in a sense of things dared and achieved together, there remains enough to keep man occupied and contented between the two dark poles of birth and death. What lies beyond that, since it can never be known, it seems unprofitable to question. Meanwhile, Life lies all around us, teeming with opportunities. Sufficient to the day are the day's eager chances. Let us take them as they come, with a frolic welcome, with " the throbbing heart's high courage," with " the unshakeable dauntlessness of human kind." They will repay the enterprise.

RUPERT BROOKE AND THE WAR

FROM time to time, in history, in politics, in literature, a single figure stands out as harbinger of a new movement, its first articulate voice and inspiration ; and Rupert Brooke must clearly take his place among these shining pioneers. It would appear that the man himself was more significant than anything he produced ; the novelty of his apparition rendered him conspicuous, but he was further enriched with the virtue of a radiant personality. All his friends loved him ; and, though the publication of what will probably have to rank as the authoritative " Memoir " does not indeed do much to explain his charm to those who were never privileged to know him, there is sufficient evidence, both there and elsewhere, that he possessed in a remarkable degree the capacity of fascinating both old and young alike. It was to the young, however, in particular, that he presented himself as the embodiment of a new ideal. For Rupert Brooke was the modern high-priest of the faith of self-realisation and independence, and his letters bear abundant testimony to the bright vigour of his influence.

It is scarcely fair, perhaps, to judge a man by his correspondence, for every sensitive letter-writer is apt to reflect in his letters the temperament of the friend to whom he is writing. And since, to Rupert Brooke's friends, Rupert Brooke himself was clearly the most alluring of topics, it is not unnatural that he should have pursued that topic with all the relish possible to a self-absorbed and concentrated individuality. He was the pet child of his circle ; and he repaid its admiration with an absolutely engaging frankness. It is to be supposed that he loved where he was loved ; that he repaid unselfish sympathy in its own golden coin ; but the best of his enthusiasm, so far as his quoted letters reveal it, is quite ingenuously reserved for himself. Just as Dickens loved to pose as " The Inimitable," so Brooke, with disarming sincerity, seems to have taken it for granted that his own personality must needs be the theme nearest to his correspondent's heart.

In this, above all things, he was representative of that eager, rebellious generation which was emerging into action at the moment when the war broke out. The spirit which he represented was a spirit of compensating revolt. The progress of civilization reveals a regular recurrence of eras of construction followed by eras of revolution. The Victorian era lasted a long time—a little too long, no doubt—and its spirit was conscientiously constructive. Victorianism bent every energy to the manufacture of a moulded and composite citizenship ; its primary object was the sinking of the individual in the mass. Arnold's Public School system (now menaced upon every side) ; Mill's utilitarianism ; Tennyson's " self-reverence, self-knowledge, self-control " ; Browning's *palæstra* of the emotions ; all the gods of Victorian poetry and ethics drove their chariots in the same direction. Their goal was self-repression and social altruism. The logical outcome of such an ideal, extended to the edge of decay, is visible in the Germany of the present hour. When general personality is undermined, power falls into the hands of a few arrogant autocrats, and an entire generation is very swiftly sacrificed. Against such a menace Brooke, and those who stood with him, rose in emphatic protest.

They stood for the rights of the individual against the tyranny of convention. They hated with a bitter hatred all prettiness and all pretence. The natural issue was an alliance, partial if not complete, with the sincerity of ugliness. Brooke's biographer insists that the school, which the author of " A Channel Passage " represented, detested ugliness; but, if it did, it detested it, like the man in Plato, with a loathing that was at the same time an irresistible fascination. " Eyes ! " it might have exclaimed. " Wretches ! take your fill of the lovely sight " ; and before the attraction was exhausted, it would have dipped its hands wrist-deep into the filth that lay by the wayside. This strange fascination is more apparent, perhaps, in the fiction of the time than in its poetry; but it disfigures the poetry as well. It sprang from a perverted desire to deal honestly with life, and to present everything that could be presented of the uglier aspects of love, and passion, and disillusionment. And the canker at the heart of the movement was an inveterate spirit of selfishness.

That selfishness stands self-revealed in its common attitude to love. The literature of this particular school is indeed full of " love " ; but it is a love rooted and grounded in self. Like Tennyson's Tristram, the lover is so detached from the loved one that, even in the moment of realization, he can hold her at arm's length, and feed his fancy with pictures of a future day, when her natural charms will have faded, and her poor armoury of sex will have fired its last ineffectual bolt. He is half afraid of Love, for fear of the disillusionment that may follow upon possession. He offers no sacrifice himself, but expects everything to be laid in submission at his own feet.

And this (we can now see clearly) was only the first step in an unconsolidated advance from the common altruism of the last generation. Individuality was emerging, as by the law of recompenses it was bound to emerge ; but it had not yet come to terms with its own conditions. Fate cut short the life of Rupert Brooke before he had built himself a citadel of the soul ; he was still wandering between the poles, when all wandering was suddenly brought to a close. His poetry, no less than his letters, shows him to be uncertain of his bearings—an uneasy mocker, concealing behind the veil of ridicule a growing fear that what he was laughing at might, after all, be nearer truth than he had the courage to believe. His latest poems suggest that he was finding his feet upon the rocks ; but the footprints by which he is most easily traced move restlessly over shifting sands.

Now, so much cant and humbug has been written and spoken concerning the spiritual influence of the war, that any reasonably cautious man has long since determined to keep clear of such generalizations altogether. Nevertheless, one single impression is beginning to be borne in with reiterated emphasis upon all lovers of poetry, and that impression seems to leave it indisputable that the young rebels of individualism, who have actually experienced the horrors of warfare, come back to their old environment in a spirit radically different from that with which they set out. Individualists they do indeed remain ; but their individualism, purged by revelation, has ceased to be introspective, and now directs its activity steadily outwards. One after another, they went out to fight in a mood of exalted self-consciousness ; one after another, they return with their sympathies extraordinarily widened, and with half the barriers of prejudice and false distinction swept away. This very broadening of sentiment is perhaps only a development of their revolt against popular sentimentality. The Victorian poets wrote of war as though it were something splendid and ennobling ; but as a matter of fact they knew nothing whatever about it. The Georgian poets know everything there is to know about war, and they come back and report it to us as an unspeakable horror, maiming and paralysing the very soul of man.

" Now, God be thanked Who has matched us with His hour," sang Brooke ; but that was before he had made trial of the kind of enemy that Death upon the battlefield really is. " It's a Queer Time," rejoins Captain Robert Graves, and forthwith unfolds one corner of the manifold map of warfare, crowded with movement, and dizzying with confusion. " War is Hell," he concludes ; and Mr. Siegfried Sassoon takes up the parable with interest. The whole purpose of his war poems is apparently the stripping of the tinsel from the robes of Bellona, the revelation of the stark and clattering skeleton beneath. All the younger poets who have turned soldiers owe to the tendency which Brooke embodied, their passion for painting war in its true colours ; but the most interesting thing about their work is the change which comes over it, when once they have lived the life of a combatant. Their sense of personality breaks the bonds of self and becomes a living human sympathy. Individualism, by one of nature's paradoxes, expands into a passion for companionship.

Take Brooke's poetry almost where you will, and the prevailing impression is one of a brilliantly attractive personality, absorbed in the contemplation of itself. Take the average poet-turned-soldier, open him at random, and the atmosphere is almost always warm and tender with a sense of the suffering of others, and the comradeship of endurance and of pain. It is even possible to trace the change in the work of the same poet. The young soldier in Mr. Robert Nichols's " Farewell " bids good-bye to his home with his thoughts still centred on his own emotions :

And now tears are not mine. I have release
From all the former and the later pain,
Like the mid sea, I rock in boundless peace
Soothed by the charity of the deep-sea rain . . .
Calm rain ! Calm sea ! Calm found, long sought in
vain.

This is introspective enough ; but Gates, the subaltern, who in the same writer's vivid and poignant " Comrades " struggles back to die with his own company in the trenches, is thinking only of the men for whose safety he is responsible, and not for one instant of himself.

And Mr. Siegfried Sassoon, the most unsparing realist of them all, finds in just the same spirit the only possible antidote to the horrors of war in the knowledge of high companionship in a great cause :

The anguish of the earth absolves our eyes
Till beauty shines in all that we can see.
War is our scourge ; yet war has made us wise,
And, fighting for our freedom, we are free.

Horror of wounds and anger at the foe,
And loss of things desired ; all those must pass.
We are the happy legion, for we know
Time's but a golden wind that shakes the grass.

There was an hour when we were loth to part
From life we longed to share no less than others.
Now, having claimed his heritage of heart,
What need we more, my comrades and my brothers ?

There is no need to labour the point ; it can be traced in almost every volume of poetry published during the last two or three years. The realistic movement has had its full chance, and it has given us in poetry the most lurid panorama of war that any art has ever achieved. Cheap patriotism and Jingo-verse may henceforth be possible to the music-hall singer ; they will no longer be tolerable in the poet. And with this realism has grown a wide-winged sense of individuality, stretching outwards to embrace all fellow-sufferers, even in an alien cause. War, which makes so little of the individual life officially, has suddenly taught the callous that the individual life is the only thing which matters. And since it was officialdom throned in high places which made this war possible, the completion of the struggle between officialdom and individualism begins to draw in sight. But the victory will not be a victory for self. The most self-centred generation in history is to be transformed into the most sympathetic and humane.

How far away the foolish, vain distinctions of five years ago appear to-day! Five years ago youth was ready to judge a man by the ties he wore, and the number of buttons upon his waistcoat. After four winters in uniform such shibboleths seem framed in a dead language. Eton and Oxford have shared the same mess with Finchley and Pimlico, and the enforced censoring of his section's letters has awakened the languid subaltern to a knowledge of the universal likeness of human nature in all the secret places of the heart. No longer parcelled out into schools and parishes, life and literature seem to promise a larger-hearted opulence, refreshed by that spirit of freedom whose pursuit has made allies of old enemies, and comrades of the hitherto misjudged and misinterpreted.

If we return, will England be
Just England still to you and me?
The place where we must earn our bread?
We who have walked among the dead,
And watched the smile of agony,
And seen the pride of Liberty,

Which we had taken carelessly
From other hands. Nay, we shall dread,
  If we return,
Dread lest we hold blood-guiltily
The things that men have died to free.
Oh, English fields shall blossom red
For all the blood that has been shed
By men whose guardians are we,
  If we return.

Should that high dream be justified by fulfilment, the feet of the young men will have set revolt upon its proper path at last. For no revolt against convention was ever of any worth until it had learnt to cast self aside, and to share its benefits with its fellow men.

STUDIES IN PROSE

DICKENS'S LOVERS

I

EVERY man, says the poet, boasts two soul-sides: and this was particularly true of Charles Dickens. There were indeed many men in Dickens, many personalities struggling one against another; but pre-eminently and in the foreground there were two main sides to his character. There was, first, the Dickens of the world of London, the man who epitomised his age, the ebullient mouthpiece of the Early Victorian era; and there was, secondly, the Dickens of the fireside, the philosopher of the simple affections, the prophet of domesticity.

And when we inquire what Dickens understood by the ubiquitous passion of Love, we get two different answers, according to which soul-side of him is uppermost at the moment. The one answer is dictated by the fashion of the time, and may be said to be already discounted and pigeon-holed. The other comes from the immortal heart of a great, simple, and sincere nature, and is the same yesterday, and to-day, and for ever. Let us strike a balance, if we can, between the two, and try to see how far Dickens leads us in the philosophy of Love.

If ever a man was the product of his age that man was Charles Dickens, and in particular he was the shining product of the life and character of London. Dickens was the giant Cockney of the forties. Just as so many of his characters are embodiments of a type, so he himself seems to embody, in Gargantuan form, the whole panorama of Early Victorian Cockneydom. And if we try to pick out a single quality as expressive of that spirit, the epithet I think which we should choose is theatrical.

The London of Charles Dickens was tremendously theatrical. Every man that imbibed its inspiration was secretly acting a part. The Reform Bill of 1832 had let loose a perfect cataract of individualism. Jack was to be as good as his master now; Mr. Roebuck was flattering the Sheffield cutlers with the glory of their independence; Macaulay was proclaiming his triumphant Philistinism: " An acre in Middlesex is better than a principality in Utopia ": young men were rollicking through the midnight streets, wrenching off door-knockers to assert their bursting personality. Steam was being let off from a million human steam-engines. The air was full of hissing and roaring. It was all one splendid debauch of the theatrical spirit. And through the midst of it revelled Dickens, the inimitable, arm in arm with half his generation.

We miss the meaning of half Dickens's character if we fail to appreciate this theatrical element. We know from Forster how it invaded his private life. The " splendid strolling " was part of it; the " garish lights " of St. James's Hall were part of it; the insatiable restlessness which eventually wore him out before his time was a pitiable part of it. But there were other sides to it less easily recognised—sides which influenced his writing even more than his conduct—and among them was his theatrical attitude to love and lovers.

Dickens's Lovers

Of course every man has a touch of the actor about him. We all like to imagine ourselves in heroic attitudes. Even if we are too sensible to set our fancies free when we are awake, what devils of fellows some of us are, to be sure, in our dreams! But the greater part of this drab, indeterminate, workaday world has very little opportunity to figure in the limelight at all. That, of course, is why the lower-middle class is so desperately in love with a funeral. Death, that dignifies the most squalid bed-chamber, brings for a few days the atmosphere of high tragedy into a mean home. For the few days that intervene between the death and the interment every member of the household has a chance, if he or she wishes it, of playing a part in the solemn drama of life. And the duller the lives into which the common tragedy of death penetrates, the keener the relish with which the opportunity is seized.

But there are other chances also, and a more cheerful opportunity for acting a part is afforded, of course, when we are in love. We all like to appear heroes and heroines to our well-beloved, however ridiculous and homely our infatuation may seem to the rest of the world. The pair of lovers under the hawthorn tree, whispering immortal nothings in the opal twilight, cannot (however sincerely they care for one another) avoid some flickering taint of the theatrical world They are living in dreams. Nobody would be brutal enough to wake them. Alas! poor dears, they will wake up soon enough of their own accord. But the wise man who overhears them in passing will smile sadly, as he goes, remembering many things.

And of all generations of whom we have any record, the Early Victorian was surely the most theatrical in its attitude to love. It did not mean, no doubt, to be insincere, but it certainly posed and attitudinised more than any sane person in our own more disillusioned age would imagine possible. It is difficult to resist the belief that the courtships of our parents were chiefly concerned with an indefatigable determination to deceive each other about their real characters and natural tastes. They must have known that they were talking the language of humbug. Surely, when they parted for the night, they must have seen through one another's disguises. And even the indomitably sincere and human Dickens was infected by the poison.

II

Let us consider one or two typical examples, and to begin with let Arthur Clennam come into the court, to answer for his loyalty towards the god of Love. He has certainly done yeoman service, for he has three girls to his name. Before the story opens he has "toyed with light loves in the portal" in company with Flora Casby. Soon after the tale is well under weigh he is musing about Pet Meagles by the riverside, and he ends up with leading Little Dorrit down the steps of St. George's Church "into a modest life of usefulness and happiness."

Arthur Clennam is, I think we shall all admit, a complete representative of the theatrical lover. His attitude to the past is theatrical. He is not half so honest as the voluble Flora, for she is true to the old sentiment, while he, it is easy to see at every turn, is terribly ashamed of his youthful infatuation.

Now, no decent man ought to be ashamed of his old loves. That is the conduct of a prig; and when Pet Meagles quite unconsciously pays Clennam out for his inconstancy to Flora by showing him that she herself is so much in love with another as never to have imagined it possible that Clennam could be in love with her—then his behaviour is even more theatrical than any modern hero of the Lyceum. For he fills the bosom of his coat with her roses (what a sight he must have looked!) and scatters them upon the moonlit river, as a sort of dramatic symbol that his hopes and dreams are floating out into the darkness. And all the while the limelight keeps playing furiously from the flies!

Are we to believe that Dickens had any faith in this sort of character, that people like Arthur Clennam and Walter Gay were created spontaneously out of the fabric of his eager genius? Surely not: or why should he have set over against them, time after time, a humble, unheroic, domestic sort of lover, with no kind of airs or graces, whose passion nevertheless goes straight to the heart, and brings the tears starting to the eyes?

Little Dorrit falls in love with Arthur Clennam; but Clennam in his magnificent, water-tight self-concentration never notices it for a moment. Who is it that notices it, then, and opens the dull man's eyes to the truth? Why, the youth who really loves her, loves her unaffectedly and unselfishly, with all the fervour of the brave little heart which swells to the size of a gentleman's under the waistcoat of sprigs—" mere slop-work, if the truth must be known "—John Chivery, son of the porter of the Marshalsea. John Chivery cuts but a poor figure on the stage of the higher drama ; but he is the perfect lover for all that, the true knight-errant among the groves of last week's washing ; and if I were little Dorrit, I would have chosen him a dozen times before the junior partner in Doyce and Clennam.

What more can love do than John Chivery did ? He loved devotedly, and without a thought of self. To be sure, he dressed himself up in all his best every Sunday when he went to pay his respects to the Dorrit household ; but then remember what an awe-struck reverence he entertained for the family honour of the Father of the Marshalsea. It was a weekly visit of state, bearing gifts—the conciliatory offering of cheap cigars, which showed that John had just enough of the wisdom of the serpent in his composition to see the advantage of squaring the father first. But that was his only touch of worldliness. For the rest, he was altogether Love's true henchman, rather weak in the legs, very weak and washed out about the hair, but at heart a very valiant knight, who, when he had learnt the hopelessness of his own suit, was man enough and hero enough to help along another's. Is there anything better in the whole of Dickens than the scene between Clennam and John Chivery, when the lad comes to open the eyes of the successful wooer to little Dorrit's secret love for him ?

Consider the intolerable patronage of Clennam and the simple honesty of young John !

" You speak, John, like a man," says Clennam, with polite condescension.

" Well, then, sir, I wish you'd do the same ! " blurts out the youth. And in a moment the truth flashes out in irresistible brilliancy.

Clennam gets the lady, of course, and seasons his vows with all the decorations of theatrical oratory, but the true honours of the Court of Love go with John Chivery. It is his solitary figure that remains in the memory, lingering on the Iron Bridge across the river, where once she used to pass o' Sundays, or composing marble epitaphs for his own tomb, among the drying clothes upon the clothes line, which remind him, by some strange perverted association, of the groves of Venus.

" He's a breaking his heart for her," says his mother, " and I could wish to take the liberty to ask how it's to be made good to his parents when bust."

How indeed ? for it is a treasure of pure gold and precious jewels !

III

Now let us pause here for one moment to ask a question upon which, I am inclined to believe, depends the whole secret of Dickens's success or failure in the pourtrayal of love and lovers.

Why is it that these simple, unheroic domestic lovers carry our sympathies with them wherever they go, while the really serious, super-fatted lovers, who were clearly designed to take the centre of the stage, trouble us not one whit, and are forgotten almost as soon as the book is closed ? Why is it ?

Well, the answer lies buried in the depths of human nature. There are two kinds of Love, Sacred and Profane : and out of Profane Love spring the great passions which have animated the world's imagination—Antony and Cleopatra, Romeo and Juliet, Henry and Rosamund—all those fiery impulses which drive a man and a woman into one another's arms, across all obstacles, and in the teeth of all the scruples of honour and advantage.

Very few men and women in a generation are capable of such a passion—fortunately for the peace of society! But every one who is in love, however mild and lukewarm the emotion which has led Angelina to prefer Edwin to Alfred—every couple in process of choosing its mate, likes to imagine that some echo of the great passions of the world is fluttering its own domestic dovecot. And so young Love gives itself theatrical airs and affectations, struts before the looking-glass, and throws itself into attitudes. And until it has recovered from these amatory measles, it is a thing of ridicule to the rest of the world.

Now, Charles Dickens was never the creator of a grand passion. There is no hero in any of his books who could declare that the world was well lost for a woman's sake. Such an idea never entered into his scheme of creation at all.

But he did, as an artist, get just so far in the pale reflection of passion as the young man who writes the sort of love-letters which make such a cruel show from time to time in the law courts. He did conceive heroes who wanted to tread the heights of rhapsody in their ladies' praise, but could never get beyond the language and the sentiment of the stage. Their hearts, in fact, were acting a part, and their tongues could only speak the language of their hearts.

We laugh at such people now; but Dickens did not laugh at them. Perhaps he did not believe in them altogether; but they were his concession to the custom of the time. So far as he could work himself into the mood, he put them on the stage with all solemnity. And there they stand to-day, the relics of a bygone generation. And the young people of our own families laugh at them; and thereby hangs a hidden truth of some interest.

There are two kinds of laughter—the laughter which laughs at people, and the laughter which laughs with people; and Dickens, who loved laughter more than most men, has plenty of both sorts and to spare. But one of the wisest things ever said about Dickens was said by Mr. Gilbert Chesterton, when he let slip the theory that Dickens, as a creator, is never quite at ease with any character with whom he has not laughed. Think of his own autobiographical novel, "David Copperfield": how he laughs with himself through all the stages of emerging boyhood, a kind, tender, indulgent laugh, that sympathises with every weakness and mistake. "What a fine fellow, I thought myself," he seems to say. "Ah me, how changed I am to-day! And yet, after all, wasn't I rather lovable in all my foolishness?" That is the true spirit of laughing with a person; and it may be said to be the touchstone by which we can test Dickens's true lovers. The people over whose romances one can smile with a fond indulgence—those are the people who really touch the heart. Dickens laughs with them, and through his laughter gleams the mist of tears—the tears of sympathy and of some fond memory of our own, which makes the whole world kin.

The more we think this over, the more convinced we become of its truth. All the lovers in Dickens whom one really loves are the lovers with whom one can laugh. Examples crowd in upon the memory, directly we begin to think. Let us recall one or two fairly obvious instances.

You cannot laugh with Walter Gay, even if you believe in him at all :

> " So, if you ever see her, uncle," said Walter, " I mean Miss Dombey now—and perhaps you may, who knows !—tell her how much I felt for her ; how much I used to think of her when I was here ; how I spoke of her, with the tears in my eyes, uncle, on this last night before I went away. Tell her that I said I never could forget her gentle manner, or her beautiful face, or her sweet, kind disposition that was better than all. And as I didn't take them from a woman's feet, or a young lady's—only a little innocent child's," said Walter : " tell her, if you don't mind, uncle, that I kept those shoes—she'll remember how often they fell off, that night—and took them away with me as a remembrance ! "

No ; it really will not pass. " Tell her how I spoke of her with the tears in my eyes, uncle, on this last night before I went away." What self-respecting man ever talked like that ? The limelight of the stage world, through which such language moves, shows up its false colours in a moment !

And what of Eugene Wrayburn, beloved of one of the most womanly women that Dickens ever pictured—trusted by the steel-bright spirit of Lizzie Hexam. Can we pass his self-conscious oratory, either ?

> Lizzie ! I never thought before that there was a woman in the world who could affect me so much by saying so little. But don't be hard in your construction of me. You don't know what my state of mind towards you is. You don't know how you haunt me and bewilder me. You don't know how the cursed carelessness that is over-officious in helping me at every other turning of my life, WON'T help me here. You have struck it dead, I think, and I sometimes almost wish you had struck me dead along with it.

Surely it will not do ! It rings false upon the counter. There is not a phrase in it that really touches the heart. The man is acting all the time, in the old transpontine fashion, with his hand upon his heart, and his eye upon the gallery.

But how about Mr. Toots ? Poor, neglected, inarticulate Mr. Toots—" It's of no consequence, thank you "—what anyone thinks of him, but he is a real good lover none the less.

Step down with Dickens from the throne of melodrama into the homely world of comedy, sit down by the fire among the people with whom you can laugh, and in a moment you are in a different world altogether.

" I'm very well indeed," said Mr. Toots, taking a chair. " Very well indeed, I am. I don't remember that I was ever better, thank you."

He doesn't know what to say to his lady. He can only gaze at her with a watery eye. Why, it is one of the first and truest symptoms of love—to be struck dumb in the presence of the beloved object.

Walter Gay, you may be sure, would not have lacked words.

" Speak like a stranger," returned Walter. " No, I could not speak so. I am sure at least I couldn't feel like one."

But it is the very essence of love, in these early stages, that it makes strangers of those who are aching to rush into one another's arms. Toots is the true lover ; and Walter Gay the false, and Toots, by all the laws of justice, ought to inherit the reward of chivalry. But alas ! the novelist could not break away from the tradition of his time. The public of the fifties would never have put up with such a marriage for their heroine as a marriage with the tender-hearted, chuckle-headed Toots. He has to be content with the maid instead of the mistress, and his good, loyal heart learns to be genuinely proud of his Susan, and the rapidly increasing family of daughters with which their blameless union is blessed. It is the common lot. How many model husbands in every generation have fallen in love with Florence Dombey, and ended by being peacefully content with Susan Nipper ! Yet the first romance is never superseded.

" I have never changed my sentiments towards Miss Dombey," said Mr. Toots, articulate and even garrulous at last. " They are the same as ever. She is the same bright vision to me always. When Mrs. Toots and myself first began to talk of the tender passion, I explained that I was what you may call a blighted flower, you know. She knows that there's nobody in the world I look up to, as I do to Miss Dombey. She knows that I consider Miss Dombey the most beautiful, the most amiable, the most angelic of her sex." What is her observation upon that? The perfection of sense. "My dear you are right; I think so, too."

There is the sublimation of married confidence. There is the secret of wedded happiness. I commend Susan Toots to the world of lovers, as a very model of wifely wisdom. Happy is the hearth that has such a plump and pleasing fairy seated in the ingle!

IV

Perhaps all this seems rather a lowering of the spiritual value of Love. Certainly the novelist of the present day finds the Profane Love of the pavement a more congenial study than the Sacred Love of the domestic hearth.

But that is just Dickens, and we must take him as we find him. The typical Victorian citizen (that was Dickens) always dominated the universal lover of humanity (that was also Dickens) to just this extent. Love to him led only one way, and that the way of respectable citizenship. The altar of St. George's Church was its inevitable goal, with the pew-opener smiling all round, the third volume of the Registers open for signature, and the fresh perspective of the street shining outside in the autumn sun. Dickens must laugh with his lovers, if he is to be truly happy in their company, and he can only laugh when a genial atmosphere of respectability lies mellow over all the world.

Give him that atmosphere, however, and that kindly hope, and the whole panorama of domestic love is spread out before you in his pages.

Think of *David Copperfield*—his book of private confessions—it contains nothing less than an odyssey of youthful susceptibilities. David begins in the nursery with Little Emily, whom he loves the moment he sets eyes upon her in Mr. Pegotty's cheerful boat-house; and the way in which that fascination floats quite naturally away, is only one in a million tributes to the novelist's wonderful human intuition. There follows Miss Shepherd at the dancing class, who was stood in the stocks for turning in her toes, received one sly kiss in the cloak-room, and was ungrateful enough for a whole bushel of brazil nuts, offered as a propitiatory gift, to prefer another youth of no merit whatever, and to make faces at David, when she passed him in the street, as a sign that all was over between them.

When we come to riper years, we do not actually make faces at our neglected flames, but the sentiment is everlasting. It is inbred in the uglier side of human nature.

And then the eldest Miss Larkins—who was no chicken, for the youngest Miss Larkins was not that,—the eldest Miss Larkins who flirted with officers, allowed David to steal a flower from her bouquet, and was all the time engaged to Mr. Chestle, a portly hop-grower in Kent; Mr. Chestle, who spent the evening of his inamorata's infidelities playing whist in the anteroom, plumply content with the certainty that she would be bound to him hand and foot in a fortnight. Excellent Mr. Chestle, and irresistible Miss Larkins! Who of us, looking back into his own secret record, would not be forced to confess to at least one Miss Larkins of his own?

But Dora, the despised, it may be, of our too reasonable younger generation! Dora is the masterpiece in the gallery of young love. Every man falls in love with Dora some time in his life. Some men are lucky enough to escape the peril of marrying her. When the ring is sent back in a despairing note, folded like a cocked hat, the dismissal, in such fortunate cases, is taken as final. That man has got free with a happy memory, and may thank his stars for his escape. Some men again fall in love with Dora after they are married to Agnes Wickfield, and they are lucky too; for there is no taint of vice in Dora's composition. She would just shake her curls in the married man's face, and skip away with Jip down the garden path. And that man, too, would have a happy memory to carry back to his sheltered fire-side, with Agnes darning innumerable stockings in the lamplight.

The really unlucky man, of course, is the man who carries Dora home, when the honeymoon is over, and settles down with her to a life-time of underdone veal and leathery pudding. For his dream is bound to be overclouded with reality; his romance inevitably melts away, when the oysters are unopened, and there is no knife to open them, and Jip has got all his feet into the mushroom ketchup. Yes, the truth is that there are some very lovable lovers who are not made for marriage, nor destined to domesticity; and it is really too bad of Dickens to make us men fall in love with Dora, only to remind us in the next breath that his beaten pathway to the steps of St. George's Church is not, after all, the only path through which Love steals its way.

Nevertheless, it is the one way for Dickens, the imperturbable British citizen ; for house-keeping, the setting-up of a home, its furnishing, equipment, and management are always the longed-for haven of all his romances. The failure of David and Dora's married life is simply a failure in house-keeping. They never loved one another less, nor went philandering after other people. Dora was a divine sweetheart to the last ; and yet she knew that her married life was a tragedy.

" I am afraid it would have been better if we had only loved each other as a boy and girl, and forgotten it. I have begun to think I was not fit to be a wife."

Well, it depends upon what you ask of a wife. At any rate, Dora was not fit to be a housekeeper.

And to be a good little housekeeper is, as we have seen, the one goal to Charles Dickens of all soft whisperings in the twilight. The lovers begin with that ideal from the first. Ruth Pinch makes a pudding, and is immediately ethereal-ised. Traddles's first consideration, when once he has secured the affections of " the dearest girl in the world," is the provision of furniture. Sophie buys a flowerpot and stand for the par-lour window out of her earliest savings, and Traddles himself acquires a little round table with a marble top—two feet ten inches in cir-cumference—" admirable piece of workman-ship, firm as a rock "—but there is always one anxiety in the background, one menacing kill-joy of apprehension. How will they ever collect the table-cloths, the pillow cases, the ironmongery and candle boxes, " because all those things mount up ? " Still their motto is " Wait and Hope."

And when the household gods are collected, even if the whole supply of family glass amounts to no more than two tumblers and a custard-cup without a handle, what a time they will have together, with their family about them, round the Christmas fire ! All roads lead at last to the roast goose and speckled pudding of the Cratchits —there was a housewife for you, if you like. " Bob said, and calmly too," that he regarded that pudding as the greatest success achieved by Mrs. Cratchit since their marriage. Come, then, let us all sit down together and be happy. The compound in the jug is simmering : the chestnuts are sputtering on the fire. " God bless us everyone ! "

Good cookery and contentment, what more has Love to ask of this generous son of England ! But there must be contentment and an honest heart. That is the essence of the bargain. The cookery at Mr. Merdle's mansion was superb, and the gorgeous butler dispensed the rarest vintages. The Bosom at the end of the table displayed to the utmost advantage the jewels which Mr. Merdle had hung upon it. That was all he wanted it for, and it performed its share of the contract in a perfectly sound and businesslike fashion. But Mr. Merdle sat at his end of the table, sunk in his chair, crumbling bread, and eating not more than eighteen penn'orth of his own sumptuous repast. For he had played Love false, as he was still playing Life false every day as it passed ; and Mr. Merdle's complaint was just that deadly disease which devours all those who betray the noblest impulses of life.

And what is more—the Merdle household is typical of that sort of marriage in which each party to the contract has a different ambition and pulls in a different direction.

Mr. Merdle wanted peace and quiet: Mrs. Merdle wanted Society, and because she always got what she wanted, her husband was dragged down the ladder of trickery and deceit until he ended in a suicide's fate, "the greatest forger and thief that ever cheated the gallows." If only Mr. and Mrs. Merdle could have effected a compromise; if only they had studied the example of the excellent Mr. and Mrs. Boffin. What a contrast between Mrs. Merdle's mansion and Boffin's Bower.

Here is a married couple, thoroughly devoted to one another, who have solved for ever the secret of compromise. There they sit, facing one another in a paradise of perpetual harmony. One half of the room is furnished like a tap-room, wood settle, sanded floor, veal and ham pie on a shelf above, pipes alight and toddy steaming; the other half is all glorious within, clothed in a flaming carpet, decorated with stuffed birds and waxen fruits. In the one half sits Mr. Boffin in *déshabille*, in the other rests his spouse in feathers and flounces. Neither envies the other, nor blames the other for any difference in taste. The vulgarian and the highflyer have found a common resting place. Oh, Harmony Jail! Is there any truer allegory of the inestimable virtue of splitting the difference?

Dickens's Lovers

V

Well, we have reduced Love and married life into the region of Burlesque. It is time to rescue it before we finish. And, of course, amid all these saturnalia of good citizenship there are glimpses enough in Dickens of the sinister side of passion —the shadow cast by Love, like the shadow which followed Betsey Trotwood through the midnight streets, or waited for Lady Dedlock by the gate of the graveyard. Dickens may not have drawn a grand passion, a supreme attraction that turns men and women into fallen gods, knowing good and evil, but he knew the ugly side of Love only too well. He knew what a beast Love can make of a man, when desire is thwarted and pride set down.

Bradley Headstone is perhaps the nearest Dickens ever got to the pourtrayal of a man tortured out of endurance by a passion which burns him like the shirt of Nessus.

" You are the ruin of me," he cries to Lizzie Hexam, " I have no resources in myself, I have no confidence in myself, I have no government of myself when you are near me or in my thoughts. . . . No man knows, till the time comes, what depths are within him. To some men it never comes ; let them rest and be thankful. . . . You could draw me to fire, you could draw me to water, you could draw me to the gallows. . . .But I have been set aside and cast out. I only hope that I may never kill him."

The step from fear to brooding, from temptation to consent is a very narrow one. Given the opportunity, and Bradley Headstone becomes

John Jasper, and jealousy finds its inevitable end in betrayal and murder.

And there are other shadows too, shadows less lowering and tragic, but none the less pathetic—the shadows of those who have played Love false by accepting a loveless union, and have had to pay for their treachery all the rest of their days. The Lammles, man and wife, each knowing the other's mercenary mind, deceived one another throughout their engagement. Each believed the other to be comfortably off; each proposed to live for the rest of their lives upon the other's competence. Upon the sands of Shanklin, in the earliest days of their honeymoon, they learnt the truth. They were both poor as church mice, and all that was possible for them in the future was to go on juggling with fortune, deceiving others as they had deceived one another, and so keep up a secret conspiracy against the world, embittered by an undying contempt for one another. What a ghastly travesty of marriage, a life bitterer than death, even the most ignoble death—the terrible retribution which Love brings down upon those who take his name in vain.

VI

But the shadows pass—all shadows always pass across the pages of Dickens's golden book of life—the shadows pass, and the sunlight comes out again. At the end of all his stories the chimes are for ever ringing the wedding peal. In the matter of Love, Dickens is an indomitable optimist, and who can say how many happy marriages crown the panorama of his dreams? The world will never forget how often he confesses in his letters the pain with which he brought every new book to a finish, and the sense of loneliness with which he released one crowd of characters after another into the world of remembrance. They had been his friends for so many months, his inseparable companions in happiness and grief. He could not bear to let them go. " Oh, my dear Forster, if I were to say half of what ' Copperfield ' makes me feel to-night. . . I seem to be sending some part of myself into the shadowy world." Over and over again we see him lingering lovingly with them on the threshold. And never more so than when the wedding bells are ringing.

For Dickens might have laughed with his characters never so much, as he followed them in and out of the tortuous ways of life, but at heart he loved them all the better for his laughter; and, " like the old-fashioned playgoer " of Cayley Drummle, he liked to see everybody comfortable and contented at the finish.

Here is Sophie, hiding behind the curtains among the dingy law-books in the Inns of Court, and dragged out into the firelight, a midsummer rose of blushes. Here, after many days, is the last bottle of the old Madeira, hoary with dust and cobwebs, the golden wine shedding a lustre on the tablecloth. For Walter and his wife have come home ; and Toots and Susan are married also ; and all the wanderings are done ; and there shall be no more sea. There must be feasting, of course, for with Dickens all happy anniversaries imply a full table ; but it shall be the simple comforts of the homely hearth—with no damaging taint of the Veneerings.

And of all such homely feasts there is perhaps one that stands out in the brightest light of all—not the less bright because it is the first feast—a wedding feast to tell the truth, and a stolen secret wedding at that. The sun is setting over the river at Greenwich, and three conspirators are seated in the bow-window overlooking the laughing water. The bridegroom is there, and, of course, the bride, and the third figure, cherubic, beaming, the very embodiment of the god of love himself, is the dear little father who has lent his countenance to this naughty runaway match, who will have to answer for it when he gets home, and who is terribly conscious at the back of his heart that he is going to be intolerably lonely now that his Bella is lost to him ; but who all the time keeps up the cheerfulness due to the occasion with his imperturbably unselfish smile.

And what a dinner it was—complete symbol of Dickensian peace—fishes of all the colours of the rainbow, dishes seasoned with bliss, and golden drinks bottled in the golden age, and hoarding up their sparkles ever since.

" You won't feel solitary or neglected, Pa, going away by yourself, will you ? "

Brave little cherub of a hero, what could he answer but " No " ? " Lord bless you ! No, my Life."

But there is no happiness in this world so complete, but it brings some shadow of loss to someone else.

" Good-bye, dearest Papa, good-bye."

" Good-bye, my darling. Take her away, my dear John. Take her home."

The old man turns back to the lonely life, as age, alas ! must always turn away, however much it loves, from the perfect happiness of youth. But the last glimpse of them is enough to comfort him on his solitary way.

For the sun is shining still ; and " So, she leaning on her husband's arm, they turned homeward by a rosy path, which the gracious sun struck for them in its setting. And, O, there are days in this life worth life and worth death. And O what a bright old song it is, that O 'tis love, 'tis love, 'tis love, that makes the world go round."

THE SWINBURNE LETTERS

THE younger generation may well be pardoned if it believes itself to be the first in the history of the world to experience such change and dissolution as have suddenly swept down upon society. It almost seems as though Revolution were now being born out of the fire for the first time, while everything that lay behind the fiery cloud of the War was hopelessly flat and stagnant. And this opinion, not so unreasonable, perhaps, in the field of politics, is now extending itself across the levels of literature as well. There is everywhere a tendency to speak lightly of old literary traditions, and to imagine that the poets whom our fathers read were mild, complacent people, who took what life offered them with open hands, and asked no awkward questions ; nay, more, that the very heart of their generation could scarcely beat for the armoury of belt and corset which protected it from the open air of nature. It is natural that an era of change and revolution should set such ideas astir ; but the theory they embrace takes simply no account of the really significant figures of the generation which is now so swiftly passing out of existence into the world of memory and record. Revolution has always been the secret spring of poetry ; and it was so no less in our fathers' time than it will be in our sons'. We have to reckon with Revolution wherever we encounter Progress.

The Victorian era (we are told it every day) was a period of stuffy, commercial ideals ; and, to be sure, it is easy enough to ridicule its smug respectability ; its confidence in the judgment of crowded meetings ; its belief in a parliamentary or municipal vote as a sort of passport to paradise ; even its intense anxiety about the survival of its own personality after death. These selfish interests, no doubt, were the common food of the common people ; and Victorianism, so far as it stopped short at these, is already dead and discounted. But much of the literature, and in particular of the poetry, which rendered the Victorian era illustrious, was at heart nothing less than a vigorous protest against this very spirit of the time ; it was as much the voice of rebellion as the youngest and the freshest voice in any new Georgian choir to-day. We need to remember this, if we are to understand Victorian poetry at all ; and posterity is having the way of understanding made clear for it by the singular good fortune which has befallen many of the great Victorians in the choice of their biographers and apologists. The art of biography, it is safe to say, was never more soundly practised than it is at the present day ; and no leader of our time has had richer fortune in this respect than that wayward, elusive, but thoroughly lovable genius, Algernon Charles Swinburne. His " Life " has been written with admirable candour and communicative sympathy by his friend, Mr. Edmund Gosse ; and now under the same care, with the co-operation of one of the most discriminating of bibliophiles, his "Letters" are given to the world in two well-equipped and annotated volumes.* The efficient performance of such a task is much more than a service to Swinburne's personal memory. It is, in effect, the preservation of the spirit of a great literary movement, the record of a potent and stimulating ideal. And it should do much to clear the atmosphere of criticism, and to explain to a hurrying generation the debt which its own happy emancipation owes to the pioneers of a period that can certainly never be justly dismissed with any glib suggestion of self-sufficiency or supineness.

We look back, then, upon the Victorian era, and we see it almost absurdly disturbed by problems of commercial and scientific progress. The political speeches of the time suggest that the good citizen's prevailing ambition was to possess an income a little more comfortable than his neighbour's; while the theological arguments of his Sunday pulpit were feverishly absorbed in buttressing the authority of the Old Testament against the disconcerting revelations of Darwinism and geology. Even poetry could not afford to let these weighty questions go by default; and nearly ten of the most active years of Tennyson's production were consumed in a noble effort to reconcile the doctrine of evolution with a belief in the immortality of the soul. But it should be noted that Tennyson was the only great Victorian poet to commit himself freely to a compromise with Victorianism. The rest were more or less openly in revolt; and none more emphatically

* "The Letters of Algernon Charles Swinburne." Edited by Edmund Gosse, C.B., and T. J. Wise. In two volumes. London: William Heinemann.

so than Swinburne himself, that brilliant Puck of the meadow of asphodel, that " flame of fire," whose lively heels beat a tarantella upon the polished boards of tradition and respectability, and then danced off into the woods of imagination among the gods and goddesses of a purely pagan paradise. Swinburne was the irrepressible spirit of mischief, which broke up the solemn Wordsworthian tea-party—" all silent and all damned." He was the harbinger, in the guise of a reactionary, who threw open the gates of freedom to the ungrateful revolutionaries of to-day.

The violence of Swinburne's rebellion is emphasised by its contrast with his descent. He was born in the very centre of tradition, the cadet of an old English family who, in his own words, " had given their blood like water and their lands like dust, for the Stuarts." " I think," he says, in a highly suggestive autobiographical letter to Edmund Clarence Stedman :

> I think you will allow that when this race chose at last to produce a poet, it would have been at least remarkable, if he had been content to write nothing but hymns and idyls for clergymen and young ladies to read out in chapels and drawing-rooms.

That would, indeed, be so ; and yet the product of the youthful Swinburne sufficiently belied his birth and education. His entire training was in accordance with the typical British tradition. For school he was sent to Eton—surely of all Public Schools the guarded home of the conventions, whence in due (or rather undue) time he proceeded to Oxford, where the adoption of an easily recognisable attitude to life and thought is (or at any rate was) the only passport to success. Yet, from boyhood onward, Swinburne was absolutely impervious to the conventional atmosphere. " He has always wanted discipline," said Professor Saintsbury, " who has never wanted music or eloquence " ; and from the outset the things that most people cared about were matters of no consideration to him. He appeared at Eton clasping a volume of Bowdler's " Shakespeare " under his arm ; and he continued, in sheer and simple independence, to defy the time-honoured traditions of the place. He liked riding, and swimming, and reading, so he rode, and swam, and read ; he cared nothing for the discipline of the cricket or football field, so he simply did not play. The work that interested him he did with a will, and was " sent up for good " for Greek elegiacs ; but most of the school routine was a weariness of the flesh, and he preferred to read the Elizabethan dramatists under the trees by the river. He disobeyed his tutor, and shook his red-gold locks in the face of authority, so that before he was seventeen he had disappeared from the school-list. Thence, after an interval, he passed to Balliol, and condescended, in a mood of compromise, to take a second in Mods. in days when few men read for Honours. But when he entered for the Newdigate, he declined to accept the obligatory restriction (laid down in Sir Roger's will) that the exercise should be written in the heroic couplet, with the result that, although he sent in what must have been one of the best copies of verse ever submitted for the prize, the judges had no option but to rule him *hors concours*. Meanwhile he was continually at issue with the authorities, and, although Jowett appreciated his quality, and did his best to save him, the preponderance of adverse judgment was overwhelming. " My Oxonian career," he wrote himself, " culminated in total and scandalous failure " ; and he left Oxford with a mild contempt for all that it stands for, and never consented to be reconciled to its standards.

It is towards the close of his Oxford career that his correspondence now published introduces him to the public ; and it displays him in the liveliest rebellion against everything that the Victorian age held most sacred. Above all, it displays him as a fervent and convinced reactionary.

The divine discontent with present surroundings, which has commonly proved the hall-mark of genius, must obviously take one of two directions : it must issue either in revolution or in reaction. And with Swinburne, as with the Pre-Raphaelite friends whom Oxford made for him, reaction was the dominant rule of life. They regarded themselves as hemmed in upon every side by smug pretence and materialism unashamed ; and they turned back to the freedom of the past, in quest of a healing inspiration for the future. Their pictures reflected the simple piety of the Flemings ; their poetry was haunted by visions of a dimly romantic mediævalism. And the first ambition of their art and poetry alike was to be honest about the primary springs of emotion ; to return to nature for a method and a creed ; and to realise the value of individual character, instead of concentrating upon the preservation of a type. The inevitable outcome was that the pedants and the prudes were shocked ; and there lurked, perhaps, an underlying, malicious pleasure in the process of shocking them. The very earliest of Swinburne's published letters revels in the entertainment:

> One evening—when the "Union" was just finished—Jones and I had a great talk. (Spencer) Stanhope and Swan attacked, and we defended, our idea of Heaven—viz., a rose-garden full of stunners. Atrocities of an appalling nature were uttered on the other side. We became so fierce that two respectable members of the University—entering to see the pictures—stood mute and looked at us. We spoke just then of kisses in Paradise, and expounded our ideas on the celestial development of that necessity of life; and after listening five minutes to our language, they literally fled from the room! Conceive our mutual ecstasy of delight.

From "a rose-garden full of stunners" to the free celebration of natural passion was a short step, after all; and the honest recognition of animal impulse was one of the first bombs to be thrown into the camp of Victorian self-deception. Swinburne and his friends recognised that the majority of the people among whom they moved accepted for the sake of respectability a religious tradition which they had never had the courage to test; and the earliest advance upon the road of honesty was a frank return to a natural paganism, sanctioned by emotions common to the whole human race.

> Wilt thou yet take all, Galilean? But these thou shalt not take:
> The laurel, the palm, and the paean, the breast of the nymphs in the brake.

To Ruskin's prudent apprehension that the youthful Swinburne is plunging into a stream of religious anarchy, the poet makes an absolutely sincere and unaffected reply :

> You speak of not being able to hope enough for me. Don't you think we had better leave hope and faith to infants, adult or ungrown ? You and I and all men will probably do and endure what we are destined for, as well as we can. I for one am quite content to know this, without any ulterior belief or conjecture. I don't want more praise and success than I deserve, more suffering and failure than I can avoid ; but I take what comes as well and as quietly as I can ; and this seems to me a man's real business and only duty. You compare my work to a temple where the lizards have supplanted the gods ; I prefer an indubitable and living lizard to a dead or doubtful god.

By " dead or doubtful god " Swinburne implied, as his letter to Stedman reveals, any sort of personal deity such as contemporary interpretation of the Bible set before its congregations. Like so many thinkers both before and after him, he had passed into a kind of theistic nihilism through the gate of precocious devoutness.

> Having been as child and boy brought up a quasi-Catholic, of course I went in for that as passionately as for other things (*e.g.*, well-nigh to unaffected and unashamed ecstasies of adoration when receiving the Sacrament), then when this was naturally stark dead and buried, it left nothing to me but a turbid Nihilism ; for a Theist I never was ; I always felt by instinct and perceived by reason that no man could conceive of a *personal* God except by crude superstition or else by true supernatural revelation ; that a natural God was the absurdest of all

human figments; because no man could by other than apocalyptic means—*i.e.*, by other means than a violation of the laws and order of nature—*conceive* of any other sort of Divine person than man with a difference—man with some qualities intensified and some qualities suppressed—man with the good in him exaggerated and the evil excised.

He saw the gods of various nations employed for shameless political purposes—one, perhaps, patriotic, another cosmopolitan; and he sought refuge in the honest acceptance of the human instincts, impelling a man to recognise his overmastering humanity. Here, at least, there seemed a natural sanction for natural self-realisation.

A consistently good Christian cannot, or certainly need not, love his country. Again, the god of the Greeks and Romans is not good for the domestic (or *personal* in the Christian sense) virtues, but gloriously good for the patriotic. But we who worship no material incarnation of any qualities, no person, may worship the Divine humanity, the ideal of human perfection and aspiration, without worshipping any god, any person, any fetish at all. Therefore I might call myself, if I wished, a kind of Christian (of the Church of Blake and Shelley), but assuredly in no sense a Theist. Perhaps you will think this is only clarified Nihilism, but at least it is no longer turbid.

These absolutely sincere expressions of faith and unfaith explain, more clearly perhaps than anything in Swinburne's poetry, the pagan celebration of the flesh which proved so revolting to the earliest critics of "Poems and Ballads." They explain at the same time the extreme, and almost Rabelaisian, plain-speaking of certain of his letters. If the dictates of the body are natural, it is at least consistent to acclaim them as honourable ; and, if that is once granted, there need be no unnecessary shame over perfectly normal processes. Nevertheless, Swinburne was to learn, at the hands of popular criticism, that his contemporaries were simply bound to misunderstand his disconcerting frankness ; and these letters bear suggestive evidence to a maturer anxiety lest he should be misunderstood and misinterpreted. " I have been more bewritten and belied than any man since Byron," he writes ; and he retained just enough consideration for " the ungainly wise " to be willing to protect his own reputation. When he had quarrelled with his publisher, John Camden Hotten, Swinburne recalled to memory certain earlier writings of a violent character which he did not desire given to the world ; and the emphasis with which he begged his friend Howell to recover them is in itself an interesting concession to propriety :

I should, of course, not like any scrap *signed* with my name, which, in the dirty hands of a Grub Street libeller, might be turned to ridicule, or to any calumnious or vexatious purpose, to fall into such hands if such an accident could be avoided. Neither Hotten nor for that matter any man alive, has in his possession anything from my hand for which I need feel shame or serious regret or apprehension, even should it be exposed to public view ; but without any such cause for fear or shame, we may all agree that we shrink, and that reasonably, from the notion that all our private papers, thrown off in moments of chaff or Rabelaisian exchange of burlesque correspondence between friends who understand the fun, and have the watchword, as it were, under which a jest passes and circulates in the right quarter, should ever be liable to the inspection of common or unfriendly eyes.

This, after all, is a perfectly reasonable apprehension; for the rest, the Swinburne Letters will reveal to many readers for the first time the absolute sincerity and almost innocent reliance upon natural instinct which, although it must be admitted to have landed Swinburne in awkward places, is at least a triumphant defence against any suggestion of that wilful nastiness or ogling relish, which lay only too often in wait behind the veil of Victorian secretiveness.

Anything like bad taste was, indeed, utterly repugnant to Swinburne's character; and while he was always a great fighter, he invariably fought like a gentleman, and hit above the belt. "It gives a zest," he wrote, "to the expression of sympathy to have some points of amicable disagreement"; and, even where sympathy had waned, and disagreement ceased to be amicable, it was the part of chivalry to observe the common decencies of tourney. He hated meanness, and despised that kind of gutter journalism which feeds upon innuendo. A letter of his to Thomas Purnell is an eloquent testimony to his manly detestation of all such corruption of the Press. He had been asked to contribute to a new "satirical journal," in the interests of a friend; and he was, as usual, ready with generous assistance. At the same time, he sounded a note of friendly warning:

It implies no impeachment to my confidence in your own good taste and sense if I say as between ourselves that but for my personal knowledge of you

I should certainly hesitate—or rather, to be quite frank, I should at once decline—to be concerned in any way with anything in the nature of a "satirical journal," especially if there was any breath or hint in the matter of any such connexion or reference as you mention, in earnest or in fun, for satirical or for social purposes, with the name or shadow of the name of any "scion" of royalty. From the "Tomahawk" down to the "Hornet," I understand such papers of late years have always sooner or later gone into ways on which I should feel it impossible for a gentleman to keep them company without forfeiting his self-respect.

His own newspaper controversies, it is true, were occasionally bitter to the limit of incivility; but it was always his opponent's *views* that he ridiculed, not his personality, nor his private history. He had a peculiar aversion from that form of personal journalism which was very prevalent in the 'seventies of the last century, and he denounced it with full fervour.

We are wont to boast that in point of literary manners we have got far ahead of the days of "The Dunciad." It is full time for us to look well to it that we do not fall behind them. This is neither the first nor the tenth nor the twentieth time that I have had to remark how far worse than in the worst days of the past would be such a condition of letters as seems really and rapidly to be coming upon us; when every liberty is conceded to every blackguard whose unwashed fingers will not shrink from grasping it, and every gate of retaliation or chastisement is closed against every man of other than the blackguard's breed.

The reader will surely agree that there is gradually emerging out of these random quotations from Swinburne's correspondence a figure refreshingly at variance from the popular conception of the fiery celebrant of strange passions and political violence. The truth is, of course, that Swinburne's reaction was a reaction not only of art, but of the soul ; and that it riveted its loyalty upon the past out of an even more stirring loyalty to the spirits of sincerity and strength. His strongest impulsion, as Mr. Gosse remarks, came from literature ; and, while " he lived in perpetual converse with the Muses," two special periods shared his heart of hearts. In the Greek drama he found perfection of form, an insistence upon the overwhelming power of Fate, and an abiding sense of the splendid endurance of foiled and suffering manhood. In the Elizabethan drama he was cheered by the fresh, shrill atmosphere of adventure, the irresistible manliness, the ready acceptance of the day's fortune, good or evil, love or death. And while his influence was reactionary, his was at least a reaction to consolations befitting a *man*, clear-eyed and firmly-set against every onslaught of an adverse fate. From the Elizabethans, in particular

> those giants who unfurled
> Their sails against the morning of the world,

he learned the imperishable virtue of friendship ; and his early letters abound in the enjoyment of comradeship, and in the noble pleasure of praise. " Swinburne was the only critic of our time," says Mr. Arthur Symons , " who never, by design or accident, praised the wrong things " ; and, whether that be unquestionably true or not, it is at least certain that his was over and over again the first authoritative voice raised in honour of work that has since stood the test of time. Such praise could only proceed from a nature impeccably free from any taint of jealousy. " I am glad," he wrote in his old age,

> I am glad you like my dedication of the book now in the printer's hands, and glad to know it recalls your own early regard for my own earlier poems ; but more especially glad if any verses of my writing may help to disprove the foul tradition of jealousy as natural among workers in our own or any other form of art. Was not that always incomprehensible and incredible to you as a boy ? It always was to me.

Friendship and admiration indeed flash out, like jewels, all over Swinburne's warm-hearted correspondence ; and there is wonderfully little blame to balance his generous gifts of praise. One eminent Shakespearean, to be sure, never fails to draw his fire ; Griswold, the traducer of Poe, comes in for a few biting phrases ; and there is a single poignant letter which refers, more in sorrow than in anger, to an old friend, now gone astray, who does not hesitate to malign where once he loved. But these are exceptions, and the general evidence of the " Letters " is a triumphant vindication of the goodwill and sympathy with which the great artists of that period pursued their art—sincerely, for its own sake, and with very little thought of gain. The commercialism of an age of " Self-Help " never tainted the Pre-Raphaelite Brotherhood. In some of the early letters Swinburne suggests a natural anxiety about ways and means. He is continually short of cash, and at a loss to turn his talent into marketable uses:

> I wish I *had* anything to do besides my proper work if I can't live by it. Which it's very well to pitch into a party like brother Stockdolloger, but what *is* one to do? I can't go to the Bar; and much good I should do if I did. You know there is really no profession one can take up with and go on working. Item—poetry is quite work enough for one man. Item—who is there that is anything *besides* a poet at this day except Hugo? And though his politics is excellent and his opinions is sound, he does much better when he sticks to his work and makes Ratbert and Ruy Blas. *I* don't want to sit in (a) room and write, gracious knows. Do you think a small thing in the stump-orator line wd do? or a Grace-Walker? Seriously what is there you wd have one take to? It's a very good lecture but it is not practical. Nor yet it ain't fair. It's bage.

There is a little of this sort of thing at first (often touched, as this is, with jovial explosions of Dickensian humour), and occasionally the poet is driven to solicit the aid of friends, such as Lord Morley and Mr. Theodore Watts-Dunton, to carry through business negotiations for which he has neither the patience nor the taste. Upon the whole, however, the most conspicuous quality of the entire correspondence is its absorbed concentration upon purely literary interests, and its complete detachment from the incidents of outside life. Fifty years are covered by the "Letters," a half-century of crowded events, war, revolution, reform, discontent, and dreams. Hardly an echo of it all, however, falls across Swinburne's messages to his friends. You seem to see this little company of enthusiasts, turning away from the present with its confused, discordant voices, and fixing its imagination upon a past which was at any rate good-hearted and sincere. There they found the fine examples of good workmanship, rich colour, and high thought, with which they strove to give their own work an equal meaning for posterity. " If you have anything to say," said William Morris, " you may as well put it into a table or a chair " ; and what he meant, of course, was that good design and good material, whatever the medium, must always ennoble the intellect of those who live constantly in its company. The first essentials were sincerity of workmanship and beauty of form ; and it was to these that Swinburne, like the rest of his friends, bent every nerve and devoted every thought. His letters abound in passages, intensely interesting to every lover of poetry, which bear witness to his vital absorption in the poet's craft, an absorption vividly coloured by what Mr. Symons has called his " French subtlety, ardour, susceptibility, his sensual and sensuous temperament." The nervous energy which he poured into his novel metrical experiments was constantly held in check by the restraining influence of the classic models by which he measured and judged every new enterprise. Metre, as one would naturally expect, is his persistent occupation.

I confess [he writes] I take a delight in the metrical forms of any language of which I know anything whatever, simply for the metre's sake, as a new musical instrument ; and as soon as I can am tempted to try my hand or my voice at a new mode of verse, like a child trying to sing before it can speak plain. This is why without much scholarship I venture to dabble in classic verse and manage to keep afloat when in shallow water.

When he was once fairly launched upon his work, he showed extraordinary rapidity, writing nearly twenty printed pages of "Atalanta in Calydon" in a couple of afternoons, and finishing them in that time so perfectly that scarcely an alteration or an addition was needed. This is the more remarkable when it is remembered, as Mr. Gosse tells us, that the physical acts of holding and wielding a pen were always cumbrous to him, and that his actual tracing of the written characters was slow. The flow of thought must have kept in full flood all the time; and he confesses that he never enjoyed anything more in his life than the composition of this poem, adding also some shrewd comments and comparisons of his own:

> I think it is pure Greek, and the first poem of the sort in modern times, combining lyric and dramatic work on the old principle. Shelley's "Prometheus" is magnificent and un-Hellenic, spoilt too in my mind by the infusion of philanthropic doctrinaire views and "progress of the species"; and by what I gather from Lewes's "Life of Goethe" the "Iphigenia in Tauris" must be also impregnated with modern morals and feelings. As for Professor Arnold's "Merope," the clothes are well enough, but where has the body gone? So I thought and still think the field was clear for me.

The artist's reasonable pleasure in good work, whether his own or another's, is not, it need scarcely be said, to be mistaken for egotism;

and the most winning of all the traits in the Swinburne " Letters " is their continual homage to achievement frankly recognised as beyond the artist's own immediate grasp. His passion for the Elizabethans was the motive force of his own excursions into dramatic poetry, and he never failed to subject his newest passages to the crucial test of comparison.

I wrote a bit of a scene yesterday between Murray and the Queen ; it is the drier political details that bother me, but without some reference to them the action (and consequently the passion) is unintelligible. I study Shakespeare constantly, " Antony and Cleopatra " especially, to try if I can learn and catch the trick of condensing all this, and cramming a great mass of public events into the compass of a few scenes or speeches without deforming or defacing the poem.

To judge oneself by the immortals indeed is no strain upon self-esteem. The gods stand firm and remote ; but one's own fellow-men are active rivals. And the refreshing quality of admiration for contemporaries is one of the saving graces of the young Pre-Raphaelites. To Rossetti, perhaps, they owed their first allegiance. He was the presiding genius of the circle ; but each was ready to learn from the others, and to acclaim each new success with untrammelled enthusiasm. Nor did they think little of their elders, after the too common custom of confident youth. Swinburne's loyalty to Landor, amounting almost to worship of the " grand old lion," recurs again and again with eager reiteration. He writes to him, protesting his " immense admiration and reverence " ; when he meets him he has " got the one thing he wanted with all his heart " ; and years after Landor's death (which assailed him as a bitter personal loss), he was for ever celebrating his poetry as " more golden than gold," and his prose as a shining exemplar before which his own showed pale and thin :

> As to the wholly unequalled if not unapproached and unapproachable excellence of his prose, you know how thoroughly I am at one with you. Indeed, it is always a thorn in my flesh when writing prose, and a check to any satisfaction I might feel in it, to reflect that probably I never have written or shall write a page that Landor might have signed.

For Landor was at once Greek and heathen—the characters nearest to Swinburne's adoration; and, though the younger poet professed himself " born and baptised into the church of Tennyson " as far back as he could remember, he was more than half afraid that Tennyson believed it possible to be " something better " than a pagan and a Hellene, " an absurdity which should be left to the Brownings and other blatant creatures begotten on the slime of the modern chaos." This energetic phrase suggests, perhaps, the proper limit of Swinburne's appreciation. An exquisite artificer himself, he not only set the very highest value upon clarity and form, he was even unnecessarily suspicious of any style that allowed itself to grow turbid or involved. Meredith's insight and humanity compelled his assent, but he could not away with the intricacy and allusiveness of his manner :

> Full of power and beauty and fine truthfulness as it is [he writes of " Beauchamp's Career "], what a noble

book it might and should have been, if he would but have foregone his lust of epigram and habit of trying to tell a story by means of riddles that hardly excite the curiosity they are certain to baffle ! By dint of revulsion from Trollope on this hand and Braddon on that, he seems to have persuaded himself that limpidity of style must mean shallowness, lucidity of narrative must imply triviality, and simplicity of direct interest or positive incident must involve " sensationalism." It is a constant irritation to see a man of such rarely strong and subtle genius, such various and splendid forces of mind, do so much to justify the general neglect he provokes. But what noble powers there are visible in almost all parts of his work !

We must, however, make an end of quotations, and enough perhaps has already been quoted to afford a fairly clear picture of Swinburne's artistic creed, and of the fresh, ardent, impassioned atmosphere in which he lived and wrote. " He suffered," says Mr. Ernest Rhys, " from excess of moral energy, a too religious sense of pity, and a too fierce, impassionate sympathy for his fellows " ; and it is a true criticism that Swinburne governed his life by his heart rather than by his head, and was always at the mercy of his fervid and undisciplined impulse. But how noble was that heart, and how sincere and generally beneficent that impulse ! It is surely one of the richest gifts of life to have loved much, and to have acclaimed one's love in language of imperishable simplicity and power.

The Victorian era (we began by agreeing) was an era of shallow commercial standards, of sham respectability, of much sad self-deception and pretence. But it was also an age of Great Men, of Heroes and Hero-Worship, and the spirit which the hero-worship spread abroad is not a spirit to be despised. No doubt, it kept the younger generation in subjection, and they have taken it out of their own world in revenge. In his dedication to that amusing and often brilliant volume of reminiscences, "Ancient Lights," Mr. Ford Maddox Hueffer, whose childhood languished in the shadow of the Rossetti-Swinburne group, declares his belief that the young people of forty years ago were oppressed to the verge of extinction by an overwhelming sense of "those terrible and forbidding things—the Victorian great figures." Life, he remembers, was for them simply not worth living because of the domination of Carlyle, of Ruskin, of Holman-Hunt, of Browning, and of "the gentlemen who built the Crystal Palace." These people, he urges, were held up to the young as standing upon unattainable heights, and yet the young were incited to believe that, if they could not attain to those heights, they might as well cease to cumber the earth at all. And Mr. Hueffer's playful advice to those who come after is simply this: "Do not desire to be Ancient Lights. It will crush in you all ambition; it will render you timid; it will foil nearly all your efforts. Nowadays we have no great figures, and I thank Heaven for it, because you and I can breathe freely."

Well: there are not many of us who need to be warned against the desire to become an Ancient Light; we are most of us only too well aware of our incapacity. But discounting the irony which gives the passage its charm, is it so very certain that the worship of Great Men is a hindering, hampering process to the mind? There was one candid and generally bitter philosopher, at any rate, who thought obliquely otherwise. "One comfort," wrote Carlyle in a memorable passage, "one comfort is that Great Men, taken up in any way, are profitable company. We cannot look, however imperfectly, upon a great man, without gaining something by him. He is the living light-fountain, which it is good and pleasant to be near." The worship of heroes has been common to all the great, emancipating periods of history, for the simple reason that, when the mind dwells in confidence upon a noble type, it has a way of catching by reflection some side-light of the nobility it admires. We should not be so ready to agree with Mr. Hueffer that "nowadays we have no great figures"; at any rate the world is alive with promise of an ample harvest of great figures in the immediate to-morrow. But there is some truth in the suggestion that the tendency of recent habit and of recent thought has bent increasingly towards the suppression of enthusiasm, towards a sort of nescience, or agnosticism, both of artistic creed and practice, towards the substitution of "mockery, that fume of little minds" in place of the whole-hearted admiration for its Great Figures which redeemed the Victorian Era from the taint of unalloyed materialism. Is the new spirit better than the old? Is a cold and empty altar to be preferred to a blind devotion? He would be a rash judge who should maintain it so.

For these men were true workers in the field of art, and even truer beacon-watchers in a night of spiritual uncertainty. The integrity of their aim and the sincerity of their ideal are absolutely impregnable. Their art was just their life. They did not court publicity in the Press; nor betray their self-respect for temporal advantage; nor intrigue for places in the "Honours List." Even the honours congenial to their craft were to them undesirable and undesired. Some eager admirer wrote to Swinburne, hailing him as the inevitable successor of Tennyson in the Laureateship. In reply he got no half-hearted repudiation:

> In the name of our common reverence and affection for Landor [wrote Swinburne] let me conjure you not to inflict on me the discredit by anticipation implied in the title of future Laureate: an office for which I expect to see all the poeticules of New Grub Street pulling caps after the death of Tennyson, till the laurel (or cabbage wreath) shall descend on the deserving brows of the Poet Close or the Bard Buchanan. For myself, I can only say of that office what Landor said:
>
> That inexpert was always I
> To toss the litter of Westphalian swine
> From under human to above divine.

Does the present generation really "breathe more freely" in an atmosphere less remote from the prevalent ambitions of the time; and, if so, is it under no apprehension lest it may perhaps be inhaling air tainted with the effluence of a crowd of paltry little men, elbowing and hustling one another for precedence at the gates of a breathless lift? At least, as we turn over once more the fresh, clear pages of Swinburne's correspondence with his friends, and are admitted to the privilege of sharing his noble enthusiasm for the high destiny of poetry, and his ultimate confidence in the even higher destiny of man, we may feel, with reverent hearts, that this indeed was how a great poet ought to speak, and live, and hope ; and that the example of such devotion to the high service of art can never be without its influence upon posterity. " Even the gods must go " ; but every generation will find its own gods for itself. The age of Great Men will never pass, so long as the artist embraces his art with the simple magnanimity of Swinburne.

THE NEW REALISM

WE are living, beyond question, in the hey-day of the young men; all the kingdoms of the world are in their hands. Thirty or forty years ago there still lingered in the social and literary atmosphere the faint mist of a tradition that experience was the one authority in life, and that youth must expect to serve its apprenticeship before it could claim the privilege of the final word. That tradition has long since dissolved and vanished. Nowadays experience is held in very modest repute; energy and initiative are the universal passports to recognition. And nowhere is this truer than in the field of literature, where, it is scarcely necessary to add, youth and rebellion have always been in a state of conflict with tradition. Until recently, however, innovation has had to fight its way; the serried ranks of criticism and convention have hindered its progress; and no doubt the opposition has done it good, by forcing each new change to justify itself before it could pass the outposts. To-day there are no outposts to pass, and experience gives way at once to the challenge of youth. It almost seems as though criticism were perpetually afraid of being accused of senility and decay, so ready is it to accept everything new, and to fall into line behind the advancing banners of youthful revolution. Like Stensgärd in Ibsen's drama, the young men of the hour may cry with confident justification: "We are young. The time belongs to us, but we also belong to the time. Our right is our duty."

But of all the regions of activity in which youth is asserting its mastery—social, political, scientific, and the rest—there is no field which it has so thoroughly made its own as that of the novel. And here the audacity of its advance is the more impressive, since the art of fiction is the one art above all others in which experience would naturally be expected to be an almost indispensable quality of the artist. For the novel seeks not only to tell a story, but to portray and moralise life ; and the neophyte, standing on the threshold of the temple, can hardly help being dazzled by the wealth and variety of the sights that stretch before his gaze. How can he possibly interpret in his first glance the virtues of the architecture or the intricate symbolism of the decoration ? Of course he cannot do so ; and the most penetrating and representative fiction of any generation will continue to be written by men whose judgment is tempered by the mellow maturity of experience.

But there are qualities vouchsafed to youth which have faded away by the coming of middle age ; and the last few years have seen a new movement in English fiction so full of vigour, sincerity, and spiritual beauty as to promise for the future, if only its edge be not dulled by the traffic of time, an entire revolution in the conventions of the British novel, clearing away a vast burden of traditional cant, and establishing a fresh and decent relation between the essential facts of life and their artistic revelation. This movement we venture, for want of a more comprehensive title, to define as the New Realism ; since the object of the realist is to draw life as it stands, and there is nothing with which these young men are so eagerly concerned as the fidelity of their art to life ; while at the same time the method upon which they set to work is altogether new, being absorbed in emotional and spiritual analysis of a deeply intimate and personal kind—a kind, indeed, which has rarely, if ever, been associated with the practice of realism in the past. It is, in effect, a New Realism of the emotions, as contrasted with the conventional realism of conditions and environment ; its interest is not the material convenience or inconvenience of life, but the spiritual achievement of man, and his ultimate realisation of his soul's possibilities. For the artist of the new realism the Kingdom of Heaven lies within the soul of man ; for the realist of the last generation it was almost invariably sought from without, in the individual's relation with the rest of the world, and in the general improvement of social and human conditions. And the advance from external consolations to the consolations of the soul is an evident advance of the highest significance and of the most hopeful promise for the future.

The struggle in literature between the real and the ideal is as old, of course, as the faculty of expression ; but in our own country, during the last century at least, the realistic novel has assumed certain clearly-defined characteristics, which may be roughly described, both in purpose and outlook, as humanitarian and altruistic. It is the natural tendency of the Englishman to work with a purpose ; his intellect being of a congenitally moral and moralising character, he likes to see even the art of his country directed towards some moral or social end. And so it has come about that behind our realistic fiction of native growth there has almost always been at work a spirit of moral indignation and reform. "Just look what our surrounding life has come to be," the realist cries in horror. "This, and this, is actually and irrefragably true!" To which the inevitable sequel follows—"This, and this, must immediately be reformed." The realism of the Victorian era was continually inspired by this sort of moral revolt.

Now it was the evils of a private lunatic asylum ; now the abuses of workhouse or foundling hospital ; at another time the slave trade, at others the prison system, the suffrage laws, the wrongs of factory workers—whatever the theme that sent the realist to his desk, his recurrent motive was the improvement of the material conditions of life. And in order to drive his moral home he developed his theme, perhaps unconsciously, through types of men rather than through personalities, while the sufferings which disturbed his peace were sufferings of environment rather than of the soul. Victorian realism, moreover, was a realism hedged in and limited by convention. Certain elementary laws of life were taken for granted ; certain moral and spiritual restrictions accepted. Whatever licence was permitted to other characters, the hero of the novel at any rate was expected to conform to the code of moral obligations laid down by society ; the ideal of life was an ideal of good citizenship, and the social standards of the State were the natural sanctions of morality. Virtue must be rewarded and vice must bring its own punishment. The traditions of the novelist's art required this happy vindication ; and any mental shocks which the reader might have sustained in the course of the story were amply compensated for by the parade of rewards and punishments upon which the curtain invariably fell.

Well, it is obvious that such " realism " was not true to life at all ; and the next step in artistic emancipation was the inevitable discovery that, seeing that virtue often gets the worst of it in this world, while the wicked man flourishes like a green bay-tree, art, if it is to represent life with any claim to fidelity, must abandon the Sunday-school prize system and face the real facts of failure and success. And so to the school of Dickens, Kingsley, Charles Reade, and the other robust stalwarts of the Victorian era, there succeeded the rather anæmic, drab, and squalid realism of George Gissing and Mr. George Moore, where incident was piled upon incident with the scrupulous exactness of an inventory, and life emerged from the picture, when its outline could be discerned at all, as a perpetual struggle against an overpowering and soul-sapping array of circumstance. The varieties of artistic temperament in the authors determined the natural varieties in the treatment ; but the main truth about this school of realism also was the fact that its interest was almost exclusively confined to the effect of a man's surroundings upon his life and character—that it was social in scope and social in atmosphere. And here, once more, the conventional standards were regarded as being so far binding upon the individual that his failure to conform to them implied an almost inevitable failure to survive in the struggle for existence. Or, at any rate, if the conventions were not accepted, it was necessary to evade them by the ingenuity of subterfuge.

The bustling, middle-class life of Mr. Arnold Bennett's " Five Towns " is pre-eminently unmoral, as it is also essentially unideal, but its citizens are quite self-sufficient and self-righteous. The squalor of New Grub Street has given way to the vulgarity of commercial success, and that success is vested in a crowd of people without imagination immensely impressed by the importance of their own petty advantages and disadvantages, the slaves of an indomitable egotism. In such an environment the wholesome human passions are stunted and deformed ; life swaggers by, unillumined by illusion and unaided by vision ; and yet, when his mean-spirited ambition sinks to a close, the citizen finds himself able to look back with satisfaction upon a career that has at least achieved as much as it set out to do. Nevertheless, what a career for " a candidate for immortality ! " The smoke of the prosperous factory chimneys hangs like a pall between earth and heaven, shutting out all conception of the spiritual capacities of the human soul.

And now, suddenly, there breaks upon the scene an entirely fresh manifestation of the novelist's art. Out of all this congested circumstance the individual emerges, alert and eager, with a wonderfully intensified sense of the value of his own instincts and emotions. He is no longer occupied with the improvement of his social conditions, for legislation and trade unionism seem disposed to settle all these matters for him without any further effort upon his part. Thrown back upon himself, and tormented by the questioning curiosity of youth, he begins to debate his own relation to his own soul, and in particular is profoundly puzzled by emotions which he finds himself impelled to indulge, while he is assured by those in authority that all such indulgence is socially and morally reprehensible. " Then," as Mr. Gilbert Cannan's hero felt, in the teeth of such a conflict between individual and public judgment,

there seemed no security in existence ; civilisation was no longer an achievement, but a fluid stream flowing over a varied bed—rock, pebbles, mud, sand ; society was no establishment, but a precarious, tottering thing, a tower of silted sands with an oozy base, blocking the river, squeezing it into a narrow and unpleasant channel. In the nature of things and its law the river would one day gather unto itself great waters, and bear the sands away. . . . Meanwhile men strove to make the sandheap habitable, for they were born on it, lived and died on it, and never looked beyond. Their whole lives were filled with dread of its crumbling, their whole energies devoted to building up against it, and against the action of wind and rain and sun. They built themselves in and looked not out, and made their laws by no authority, but only by expediency, and the young men, in their vitality too great for such confinement, knew that somewhere there must be firm ground, and were determined to excavate and explore.

It will be seen at once that we have here a very different attitude to life from that adopted by the tragic comedians of late Victorian realism; for the conflict is no longer between man and his environment, but rather between man and his fatal incapacity for self-realisation. The central motive, in fact, is idealistic, while the fashion in which it emerges in the story is congenitally steeped in realism. Sentiment has joined forces with reason, and the claims of both are frankly recognised.

Historically it might be possible to trace the origin of this new movement as far back as nineteen years ago, when Mr. H. G. Wells published "Love and Mr. Lewisham," a novel which has never, perhaps, been valued at quite its true significance. The hero of this poignant story is a young man intensely self-conscious of the possibilities of his own career, quite abnormally self-centred and vain, whose life was suddenly invaded by sentiment, and swept away from its bearings by the consequences of a young, undisciplined emotion. The experience shipwrecked his career, but the disaster made a man of him. He gained his own soul, in fact, by losing his whole world. The study is shrewdly true to fact, and yet the influence of a warm tide of sentiment pervades its every recess. It is surely not too fanciful to regard it as the harbinger of this new school of realists, working in the atmosphere of idealism, eagerly alive to beauty, keenly desirous of realising beauty in themselves, and bitterly disillusioned when they fail in a quest whose very sublimity renders it almost inevitably doomed to failure, at least partial, if not actually complete.

Youth, it must be understood, is of the essence

of the theme, for all these young men are struggling in the meshes of their own crescent temperaments, and the struggle begins as early as the schoolroom. If ever there was a citadel of tradition that stood firm it was the English public school, until the New Realism began to undermine its bastions. The English school story, since the days of " Tom Brown," has always been true to its convention. Whatever might be the conflict between boys and masters, it was taken for granted that schooldays were a glorious time, that school games were the charter of British boyhood, and that every healthy-minded boy left school in a flood of sentimental emotion, carrying with him the traditions of " the old place " to inspire the energies of manhood. The thing had been done so often that everyone accepted it as gospel ; and then came Mr. Arnold Lunn, and, with an almost offensively imperious gesture, stripped the tinsel from the old boy's imagination, laying bare the memory of many forgotten miseries, and exposing to the cold air of fact a scarecrow of middle-aged self-deception. It is to be hoped that not all modern schoolboys are quite such Philistines as the majority of Mr. Lunn's Harrovians ; but no man who is honest with his own recollection can deny the truth of much of this disconcerting counterblast to the sentiment of generations. No doubt there have been many weeks in many lives when " Harrow footer on Harrow clay " seemed a dreary servitude ; when the bloods made beasts of themselves, and tyranny flourished, and when the decent name of friendship was dragged in the mud of insipid sentimentality. But Mr. Lunn's chief claims to remembrance are the vividness with which he suggested the worried discontent of youth, as it washes to and fro, loose of its bearings, and the absolute sincerity which insisted that boys do not necessarily love the things they are supposed to love ; that most of them are much older at heart than their elders realise ; and that the only way to gain their confidence is to do something, if you can (and the best can do little enough), to help one of them here and there to realise himself, and to get his feet firm upon that particular path of life in which he is most likely to find contentment and a purpose.

Mr. Lunn, however, is no more than a half-hearted adherent of the new movement, with one foot still stuck in the clay of the last generation. Like the late Victorian " naturalists," he banishes romance altogether from his world, and romance is of the very lifeblood of the New Realism. By the sunlit stepping-stone of Mr. Ivor Brown's " Years of Plenty " we may pass into the rich summer garden of adolescence, where we open the enchanted pages of Mr. Compton Mackenzie and are made free of a new world of fluttering dreams and passions. Here, at last, is the new movement in full flower, with sincerity and beauty wandering hand in hand through a veritable Odyssey of youthful susceptibilities. The sincerity of the revelation is, indeed, its most astonishing virtue. When Thackeray set out to trace the development of a young man's soul in " Pendennis," he premised at the outset that there were some things which could not possibly be told. Art and discretion alike demanded that the modest veil of dim suggestion should be spread between the object and the spectator. But now it is enough that a thing should have happened for it to be recorded, or that a sentiment should have been entertained for it to be analysed. There is nothing vicious, we are assured, in natural emotion. Let the soul of the young man reveal itself as in the confessional; it is precisely the hidden thoughts and secret sins that make up the life of the character. Let them be faced honestly —just as they presented themselves, in fact, under the glowing excuse of irresistible impulse and youthful ardour. The hero will be untrue to his spiritual ambition; he will play fast and loose with his tenderest passions; in a whirlpool of contending moods he will be swept out of his course and come near to denying the very light by which he steers. Nevertheless, let the artist set down the whole truth; youth is the age of disillusionment; it is out of such shattered dreams that manhood emerges with a foothold and a philosophy.

"Sinister Street" is the panorama of a young man's soul in the formative years of his life. In some respects, indeed, it is like a panorama painted by a Pre-Raphaelite artist, with every detail in high relief, so full of design and colour that the main outline of the picture is apt to be obscured by its elaboration. And no doubt the book, in common with the majority of its class, suffers somewhat from the lack of structure and proportion which is inseparable from its nature. The method upon which the tale is constructed is the method of a very full and sensitive memory, which has always been influenced, not so much by the thing said or done, as by the spirit underlying the word or deed. It is a complete reversal of the old sentiment:

> No doubt it was right to dissemble your love,
> But why did you kick me downstairs ?

for to this super-sensitive sort of temperament the physical experience of being kicked downstairs would matter very little, while the spiritual betrayal of a dissembled love would matter all the world. Michael Fane's boyhood is a long tribulation of such intimate impressions, beginning with the nurse's tales of nightly horror and the cook's drunken babblings, and leading on through the passionate stirring of religious impulse, and thence by a natural transition, by way of Dora's eyes and Lily's pouting lips, to the full revelation of love, idealisation, and disillusionment. The picture is unbroken by conscious contrast and undisturbed by artifice. It simply unfolds itself, like life, in a coloured scroll of hope and disappointment.

It is still, of course, an open question how far Art should reproduce life just as it is, and how much licence may be permitted to it in the way of arrangement and stage management. George Eliot blamed Mrs. Gaskell for her love of contrast and dramatic effect, maintaining (as is indeed true) that life does not work towards " curtains," through a series of conveniently arranged episodes. Nevertheless, there is this to be said for the well-made story, that the reader never forgets its principal characteristics, while the new school of fiction does undoubtedly lose its outline in the memory within a month or two ; so that one story melts into another in a vague mist of confusion. On the other hand, such is the wealth of detail in this new spiritual realism that the reader returns to it again and again with a sense of novelty and surprise ; the emotional insight is so various, the human touches are so manifold, and the intuition is so acute as to be almost feminine. It is not astonishing, therefore, that the women characters should be just as sensitively revealed as the men. The theme is youth ; and youth is womanhood's peculiar province. Upon the artist's avowed principle that "childhood makes the instrument of life, youth tunes the strings, and early manhood plays the melody," the influence of woman in the game becomes paramount, for the boy's mother and the young man's sweetheart are, from generation to generation, the moulding measures of his character. In "Sinister Street" the manhood of Michael Fane is shaped by the process of disillusionment. He learns much when he hears the story of his mother's shame ; his education is completed when his sweetheart plays him foully false. But the disillusionment never deepens into despair. The imperishable charm of romantic passion mellows every memory. The tragedy of youth may be age, but so long as the heart is young there is always hope. The one thing youth has to dread is the withering of the receptive faculties. Life is full of adventure and recompense. Even Columbine, when her fresh innocence has been broken upon Ixion's wheel, may enjoy a St. Martin's summer of reconciliation ; even the lonely Pauline, when her lover's selfishness has tarnished her bright faith in love, can re-live the lost springtime in recollection, and revive forgotten kisses, when the roses break again along the Rectory garden-paths. Youth is born to be disillusioned, and when the process is over, youth is over also. But so long as hope revives, so long is life still worth living.

Happiness, therefore, lies apparently in illusion; and Mr. Gilbert Cannan, working in a sterner medium than Mr. Mackenzie, would extend the activity of illusion from the cradle to the grave. Life to him is always round the corner, perpetually avoiding our grasp. Like children, we take everything for granted, and find our only happiness in a game of pretence. The old parson in "Round the Corner" spends all his days in an atmosphere of the traditional concept of life, and only realises, when his pilgrimage is closing, that he has never touched hands with reality at all. In "Old Mole" the middle-aged schoolmaster is forced by the inequity of circumstance to break free from tradition, at a time when he is already too old to profit by his freedom. In "Young Earnest" a beginner in life takes his courage in both hands, and does not arrive at a glimpse of the true meaning of existence until he has splashed himself pretty considerably in the miry gutters of experience. All of them are playing with life, concealing the truth from themselves and from one another. They hurt one another in the course of their game; they do frequent and irreparable wrong to their spiritual consciousness; and yet they have their exquisite intervals, when pleasure and pain are so closely intertwined as to be almost inextricable. The most perfect moments in their life are the moments of pure emotion.

No doubt this glorification of the sensuous side of human nature is to a great extent a reaction against the false importance which the last generation ascribed to science and scientific phenomena. The very poetry of the Victorian era was not innocent of the taint of science ; the trail of Darwinism was heavy upon the contemporary imagination. Years have passed ; Science has ridden roughshod over the world and is now found to have effected absolutely nothing in the service of the soul of man. Indeed, the history of the last few years upon the Continent of Europe goes to prove that the most scientific of all nations may also be the most inhuman and brutal. What more natural than an escape from all scientific restraint into the purely natural atmosphere of impulse and emotion ? And when a great war sweeps down upon the world, revolutionising all existing standards, impulse and emotion come into their own again, as the only surviving guides of a universe which seems to have lost its way in a dark forest of spectral horror and desolation.

Before the war the youth of England might have been mistaken by a superficial critic for a body of self-indulgent, pleasure-loving, indeterminate triflers. The very fiction which we have been considering appeared to many to be little more than an apologia for a vain Epicureanism, wasting its summer afternoon among cushions and punt-poles, with Lalage's low laughter rippling across the sun-flecked waterlilies. But when the first gun sounded in the distance, most of the white-flanneled figures were on their feet, and Youth had answered once again to the call of the most sombre and disillusioning realism of all.

And, as it happens, the literature of the years of trial has furnished us with eloquent examples of the influence of war upon the New Realism, in the shape of Mr. Hugh Walpole's powerful and imaginative novels, "The Dark Forest" and "The Secret City." In the first we find a group of young men, of different types and nationalities, transported to the Russian front in the service of the Red Cross. That nothing may be wanting to the emotional complication of the case, they are accompanied by women helpers, with whom, inevitably, first one and then another falls in love. Between two of the men there lies the shadow of a dead woman whom both have loved, and in whose memory each of the survivors finds his sole sustaining inspiration. War has been often enough described in fiction before, but rarely, if ever, with such an intensity of emotional force and spirituality. The bare horror of the surroundings is suddenly illuminated by spiritual insight, so that the ghastly experiences to which this sensitive company of tyros is exposed are accepted, not as a series of inevitable physical assaults upon the nervous system, but rather as forming a beneficent threshing-floor of character, where the true is winnowed from the false. The sudden reduction of all emotions to the bedrock platform of life and death eliminates everything but the essential; all inequalities of temperament and misunderstanding fade away in the sudden revelation of immortal truth. Life, that once seemed always round the corner, is now face to face with the intrepid combatant of death.

And in "The Secret City" we may see the philosophy of the sudden collapse of civilisation most subtly portrayed under the guise of a highly imaginative symbolism. The secret city of the title is Petrograd, that home of eager dreams and bitter disillusionment; but Petrograd, in the wide panorama which the novelist presents to our imagination, stands for something at once more intimate and more universal than itself. It stands, in effect, for the lonely, aspiring spirit of humanity, the aching heart of the world. "In each man's heart," says one of his characters, "there is a secret town, at whose altars the true prayers are offered," and Mr. Walpole evolves from the Russian capital, with all the agony and frustrated hope of its last two years of history, a deeply moving and inspiring picture of the eternal solitude and thwarted ambition of those long ages which have now come to a head in revolution and chaos. The Neva, as it stands ice-bound in the centre of the city's heart, seems like a mirror reflecting the silent agony of millions upon its banks; the lowering winter clouds above the roofs and spires are heavy with the fate of a generation. The secret city is the heart of man, hoping, dreaming, baffled, broken by the blows of fate, and yet confident in itself of a final resurrection. Like the human soul, "Russia believes in the peace of the world, in the brotherhood of man, and she will sacrifice everything for it. She will go out, as Christ did, and be tortured and be crucified, and then on the third day she will rise again." . . . For the secret city is the city of eternal hope.

The book is simply packed with character.

But the distinguishing quality of the story is its atmosphere, its symbolism, its almost philosophic presentation of the ideals of a generation in travail, of a whole race sacrificed to an unattainable ideal, of a secret city of the soul that knows its own bitterness, yet guards it as a jewel saved from the dust, an amulet of promise for a not impossible future. And that note of hope lifts the novel into the realm of clear and untrammelled vision. It is typical of the movement it represents. It is not afraid to be honest, but it has faith enough to escape despair.

We hail, then, in this latest development of English fiction a definite, sincere, and successful attempt to speak the truth about the things that belong to peace of the human soul. It is definite because it breaks finally with a number of retarding conventions which obliged the novelist to muster his characters in pens, some labelled virtuous and some vicious, and both classes expected to behave in every occurring situation precisely in accordance with the label of its class. The New Realism goes straight to the heart of man, and finds it of mingled yarn, good and ill together. It is sincere again because, while it recognises the omnipotent claim of romance and true sentiment, it has banished sentimentality altogether from the stage. False romanticism is no longer permitted to veil the facts of human nature, and the shame that is afraid of the naked beauty of pure passion is nailed implacably to the counter as false coin. But, on the other hand, there is an overwhelming shame when desire, or its gratification, is allowed to become ugly. What is ugly and gross is recognised at once as disgraceful.

Tradition and Change

When Michael Fane looked into the cave by the seaside and encountered a hideous revelation of physical passion, his instinctive purity revolted in disgust. It was his first acquaintance with that prurient lust which is in reality the murky, black obverse of love, the very negation of the bright, wholesome impulses of youth. Fresh, clear passion does not hide itself in a cave. It is a creature of the open air, swift as the running brook, changeful as the sunlight that trembles through the quivering leaves. It is a fairy changeling of the moment that has nevertheless touched hands with immortality. The New Realism, after all, is only the old Idealism, seen from the other side.

THE RELIGIOUS NOVEL

THE publication of Mrs. Humphry Ward's "A Writer's Recollections" will have revived many memories, both literary and social, in the minds of those who were young and enthusiastic some thirty or forty years back; and in particular it will have stirred the embers of forgotten controversy about "Robert Elsmere" and the Oxford life of the seventies and eighties of the last century. It is difficult to realize to-day how violently that honest problem-novel disturbed the theological world of our own youth. But to the present writer there recurs a typical picture. A group of undergraduates were waiting round a lecture-room fire. The lecture was to be concerned with the "Greats" School —always a hotbed of religious argument—and somebody mentioned "Robert Elsmere," then just warm from the press. Suddenly the lecturer himself hurried through the door, overheard the last sentence, and spreading his thin fingers to the firelight, murmured pensively: "Ah, yes! 'Robert Elsmere'—a most conscientious work, to be sure; but I own that I prefer to keep my fiction and my theology in separate compartments."

The criticism was typical of the time; and it has survived even till to-day, when all the old standards of taste and judgment are being incontinently cast into the melting-pot. There are still a great many people who are in two minds as to whether a novel that sets out deliberately to discuss a religious or sociological theme can be regarded as a work of art ; and the school of criticism which decries the " picture with a story " is, rather perversely, eager to contemn the "story " which is anything more than a " picture " of manners and incident. Can the problem novel (it is asked), and in particular the theological novel, claim to stand on the same level of art as the novel of romance or of character ? Does not the trail of the homilist inevitably obliterate the proper pattern of art ? The critics of Mrs. Humphry Ward's reminiscences have returned to the attack, flying the old standards : and the question is sufficiently alive to merit a brief consideration from the dual points of view of method and effect.

Now, before such a problem can be discussed at all, we must obviously agree upon what we are to expect of a novel, if it is to fulfil its proper artistic function. And there are certain cardinal points upon which there can be no disagreement. The object of the novel, every one will concede, is to tell a story, and the story must portray human life in the clutch of circumstance. This is elementary ; and to this it may be added that the more effectually circumstance is shown to be influencing human character and moulding human lives, the more completely will the novelist be fulfilling his task. The essential quality of the sound novel is that its incidents should grow out of the clash of character with character, and that they in their turn should influence the nature of those who suffer under their operation ; so that a sort of continuous chain is established from character to incident, and from incident back to character, the whole process illustrating and explaining some hidden theory of life and conduct.

So far, it is to be presumed, every critic of creative literature will agree. We may now proceed a step farther. If incident is to grow out of character, it is clear that the central moral ideas which inspire the soul of man must provide the most fruitful material for fiction ; for there is nothing for which a man fights more stubbornly than for the ideas which he holds sacred as laws of life. And of all these ideas is there any more potent than the ruling passion of religious belief ? The entire history of humanity is splashed with the blood of religious conflict.

Tantum religio potuit suadere malorum !

Surely if the task of fiction is to display mankind in its struggle with the perils that beset its soul, there could scarcely be a richer field than that of religious difference. For religion is in its nature the secret code of the soul ; it embodies the doubt and faith for which men struggle and die ; it represents the lodestar of life to millions in every generation. For centuries it was religion which evoked the noblest endurance of humanity, and prompted no less its grossest brutality ; no shore of the world is innocent of its dead ; no nation but stands convicted in its name. Historically, in any case, it offers the novelist a practically inexhaustible opportunity.

Small wonder, then, that some of the finest historical novels in the world have religious difference for their theme. The lurid incidents of " Quo Vadis ? " the opulent imagination of " Ben-Hur," the tender transcendentalism of " John Inglesant," and the swift and intricate adventure of " The Cloister and the Hearth," will occur at once to every reader's recollection. And, as the pageant of the religious novel moves down the centuries, it will be noted that the theme grows more and more complicated by sophistry and problem. Christianity, at the outset, was a simple thing ; you took it, or rejected it, as an exercise of faith built upon immediately recorded facts. Men were still alive then who had walked with Christ, and talked with His disciples. They believed, because they had before them the evidence of those whom they trusted. Time passed ; and faith was no longer a matter of revelation. It had then, perforce, to found itself upon tradition. Legend grew up round history ; interpretation stepped in to explain ; and the multitude of interpretations confused the issue. One was of Paul and another of Apollos ; so that the struggle was no longer that of the faith against the world, but of sects and counter-sects within the faith itself, tearing it asunder with internal strife. And so the simple heroisms recorded in a novel of beginnings like " Ben-Hur " give way to the unnatural antagonisms of " The Cloister and the Hearth," and these in their turn merge into the recondite philosophical theses of " John Inglesant." Yet in all these stories we recognize without question the native activity of the novelist. No one would deny them their place among the tales that hold the imagination and stir the heart.

Where, then, are we to trace for the first time

this hidden danger which is supposed to infect the religious novel, and to remove it from the elect company of art? Probably we have our finger upon it here, at the moment when fiction ceases to deal with passion and with incident, and concentrates itself upon sophistry and argument. For sophistry is on the way to boredom; while argument wastes itself in propaganda; and when once the novel lends itself to propaganda, we shall agree that it is "on the rocks." It is not difficult to apply a rough test. So long as the theme grows naturally and by suggestion out of the clash of character, fiction is never likely to lose its head; but directly we perceive the novelist to be deliberately arranging his incidents, or grouping his characters so as to illustrate and develop his theme, we may begin to suspect him of infidelity to his art. For the art of the novel is to represent life, not to twist life into the pattern of an argument.

The ground is beset by pitfalls, and the only way out is through stringent selection. There is a passage in Mrs. Humphry Ward's "Recollections" which affords a perfect illustration of the artist's dilemma. Her "Robert Elsmere" had for its theme a situation full of dramatic promise, but none the less fraught with difficulties. It dealt with Christianity in its most modern phase, when the very authorities upon which the creed relied were threatened with annihilation. A young parson, wedded to a devout woman, was to be confronted with a general attack upon the "testimonies" of Christianity, and to feel himself forced to resign his orders. This conscientious act of his was further to estrange him from his wife, so that, prompted always by the purest motives, he was to find himself stripped in a moment of all that had hitherto made life worth living. It was a sound, dramatic situation ; but the difficulty was to keep it clear of excessive argument. The process by which Elsmere's faith was undermined must be indicated ; and yet the story should not become overburdened by dogma and attack. In working out her task, then, the artist had to abandon any amount of material, almost as soon as it was written, cutting the argument down to essentials in order to leave the narrative free and keep it dramatic. It was a genuine sacrifice, but a clear necessity of art. Yet it led to misinterpretation. For when he came to review the book, Gladstone solemnly protested against the omission of many excellent arguments upon either side, which should (he held) have been included, if the discussion was to be really representative. As though the whole duty of the novel were to reflect the close atmosphere of a parliamentary debate ! The suggestion is absurd ; yet it serves to indicate, better than any amount of theory, the main obstacle to art which tracks down the novelist who ventures out upon the slippery levels of theology.

And so far, it must be noted, the difficulty is one of pure workmanship alone : there are further and more vicious complications, if the artist permits himself consciously to lend his art as a vehicle for propaganda. The case of Monsignor Benson is a typical example. His first book, "The Light Invisible," was almost blameless artistically ; it sought to suggest an atmosphere, and was wisely content with suggestion. But, as the prison-house of sacerdotalism closed more and more darkly around him, he allowed the preacher to overwhelm the novelist ; he cast all scruples of art to the winds ; and his later books were little more than vehement tracts, urging upon their readers a thousand and one arguments for enlisting in the Roman Catholic branch of the Christian Church. It would not be easy to find a more menacing picture of the dangers that beset the employment of the novel for the direct purpose of religious proselytism.

Are we to conclude, then, that it is practically impossible for a religious novel to remain a sound work of art ? Far from it. The harder the task, the more eagerly will the artist assail it. Some of the finest literature in the world has been devoted to the cause of religion—poetry, essay, biography : why should fiction alone give up the task as insurmountable ? For the theme is at least as noble as any that the mind of man can conceive. The struggle of faith and unfaith; the misunderstanding which always trembles, like a fugitive fire, above the frank expression of belief or doubt ; the bitter animosity which religious difference breeds ; the courage of the saint and the suffering of the sinner ; these are surely among the most permanent and searching influences that sway the heart of man. Still, the artist who is to weld them into the form of fiction will need exceptional qualities. He must be detached in outlook, free from prejudice and the fever of partisanship. He must present a picture, not argue a cause. Nothing is more repugnant to the true spirit of the novelist than violent impulsion towards one side or another ; the story-teller who gets out of patience with his characters invariably alienates his readers. Again, he must select his material and fuse it with imagination ; in no other form of art is the value of suggestion more imperative. After all, the soul of man is always moved by spiritual force rather than by didactic argument. John Knox may fulminate for hours against an unimpressionable crowd ; but when a greater John than he whispers " Little children, love one another," the eyes of all the company are in a moment wet. The story-teller needs, moreover, intense human sympathy and breadth of vision, for the rocks upon which the religious spirit breaks itself are often very small and very dark indeed.

There is something ineffably pitiful, deeply and arrestingly tragic, in the misery which the spirit of man will undergo, as it struggles to attain religious peace and consolation. In that struggle humanity seems instinctively to stiffen into selfishness. There is no kind of thought which admits of such unyielding obstinacy. History tells us again and again how men have betrayed all that they loved best, at the call of some strange loyalty to a partial and broken belief which they have not even tested and found true. One man spends his energy to keep a candle alight upon an altar ; another wrecks his very vitality to put the candle out. And in their wrath one against the other, neither has time to lift his eyes above the mercy-seat to the true light that lighteth every man coming into the world. Could there be a richer opportunity to illustrate the irony of human life, the folly with which it builds up a fabric of trouble to its own destruction, the prodigality with which it scatters its benefits like seeds by the wayside ?

The strength and the weakness of man are rooted in his religious belief. It presides over the beginning and the end of his days : it hallows his going out and his coming in. The artist will search in vain for a theme worthier of his true devotion ; for over it there broods the very spirit of immortality, linking age with age, and beckoning each generation, as it passes, onward and upward into the vision and the gleam. The waste of the world and its achievement also : the hatred and the scorn ; the love and the aspiration ; the hope and despair of whole generations find their utterance in religion alone. Here is a picture of inconceivable possibilities. " Who is sufficient for these things ? " That indeed may be the question. But nobody can doubt the grandeur of the theme, if only the fit artist can be found to comprehend it.

SAMUEL BUTLER

Samuel Butler : Author of " Erewhon " : The Man and His Work. By John F. Harris. London : Grant Richards.

THE rebels of one generation become the leaders of the next ; and under the sifting, clarifying influence of time, the wisdom of Samuel Butler is triumphantly coming into its own. His public reputation has been almost entirely posthumous. During his lifetime the publication of his books, undertaken at his own expense, involved him in a loss of something like a thousand pounds ; and, while he made a few disciples who managed to achieve a certain notoriety by exercising that capacity for self-advertisement which he would have thoroughly despised, Butler himself was generally regarded as a rather amusing but inconsiderable eccentric. Since his death, however, the tide has flowed steadily in his favour. More than one valuable critical monograph has been devoted to his memory ; respectful reference to his views crops up continually in authoritative quarters ; and the recent study of his life and work, by Mr. John F. Harris, being clear and businesslike, quick in insight and sensitive in interpretation, should serve to introduce him to many new readers. And the more readers Butler obtains, the better for the intellectual sanity of the nation. For Butler always was, and always will be, a most wholesome exploder of ignorance and prejudice.

Samuel Butler

A perusal of certain recent biographies promotes the impression that the evangelical atmosphere of the average Victorian middle-class home has had a good deal to answer for. Most of the irreconcilable rebels of the last generation were bred, by reaction, in that highly respectable environment ; and Butler among them. He was a grandson of the great Dr. Butler of Shrewsbury, was born into a mild, Midland parsonage, and found himself face to face at Cambridge with the smug persistency of the Simeonites. He smiled quietly to himself, and continued on his way towards a clerical career ; but a year or two's work in a West End London parish persuaded him that the Church at any rate was not his world. Strangely enough, his first doubts were aroused by discovering that the unbaptised boys in his classes were just as good and well-behaved as those who had been received into the faith. The suspicion thus stirred stimulated others, so that he soon abandoned all thought of holy orders, and emigrated to New Zealand and a sheep farm. There he worked for five years, in comparative solitude ; and there can be no doubt that this period was the most formative in his life. He was alone with nature ; the simple life cleared his mind ; and when he returned to England, the contrast between the fresh, open existence which he had been leading, and the artificial, self-deceptive standards of Victorian London burnt into his brain like fire. Henceforth he set himself, with every argument at his disposal, to urge his countrymen to take a more honest view of life and its responsibilities, and to wash their eyes clean of hypocrisy and pretence.

Certainly the age, against whose standards he raised his protest, was steeped in a poisonous complacency. The utilitarianism of Bentham and Mill had merged into a slack policy of laissez-faire. Society was exceedingly well pleased with itself, and made its own idols of those whom it had itself crowned with material success. The whole country was dominated by the tyranny of big names, none of whom the world regarded until it had somehow become a fashion to believe in them ; while, when once they had been accepted, it was held sheer blasphemy to doubt their impeccability. Like Nebuchadnezzar of old, the age worshipped the images which it had itself set up, and required all faithful citizens to obey without question the summons of the sackbut, psaltery, dulcimer, and all the other instruments of adulation. Success was the god of the market-place ; and a withering worship of success was instilled in the schoolroom, and survived to maturity. The spirit was vigorous, and long-lived. The same commercial religion triumphed through the two Jubilees, and was not appreciably disturbed until the outbreak of the South African War, when England at last found herself up against the criticism of half the civilised world ; and the sudden light, which was let into the dark places of national inefficiency, began to flutter the self-satisfaction of the dwellers in the cave. Since then the air has grown increasingly full of questionings ; the most effectual literature of the time has been rebellious ; and the sincerity and far-sighted wisdom of Samuel Butler have begun to make their way.

Butler was indeed the exact antithesis to his

age. Instead of being self-satisfied, he was perpetually obsessed by shortcomings ; in place of self-concentration he bestowed his whole thought upon the environment which hemmed him in. " Erewhon " is a comprehensive satire of Victorian England, drawing out the absurdities of the time to their logical conclusion, in a world where, if success is the measure of honour, failure must needs be a crime, and where the man with £20,000 a year is exempted from taxation, as a tribute to the splendid imposition which he has exacted from his contemporaries. Satire was Butler's perfect weapon, but it was a creative satire, not a destructive. It was designed to help the age to rehabilitate itself by getting into honest relations with its own motives and purposes. It was, above all things, the satire of a man who has ideals, and who desires to instil those ideals into his fellow-men ; but who, at the same time, having a natural aversion from the preaching business, finds it more congenial to drive his meaning home through an undercurrent of humorous exaggeration. And speaking to the public, he spoke in plain language. He cherished an instinctive distrust for scientific jargon, and went straight for good, clear words to express good, clear thoughts. His suspicion of all religious organisations made him dislike every form of introspection and self-consciousness ; the mainspring of his ethical system was a belief in unconscious action, inspired by a naturally attuned nature. The properly harmonised character would, he believed, act morally by its own impulse ; but this impulse could only be fostered by heredity. The heredity of Butler.

however, was very different from that of Darwin, "The Origin of Species" was published while Butler was still in New Zealand, and it exercised inevitably an enormous influence over his mind. Nevertheless, he was one of the very few who declined to subscribe blindly to every detail of the theory of Natural Selection. One of Butler's first satirical essays was a burlesque application of Darwin's theory to the world of machinery, arguing that, on the principle of evolution, machinery would soon grow too strong for man, and would establish over humanity a cynical, iron despotism. It was not only a travesty of the Darwinian philosophy, but an implicit criticism of the ethical standards of an industrial age, in which the machinery of success, money, and self-advertisement had become the Dagon of the whole nation's idolatry.

Butler separated from Darwin, in short, on the border-line of Darwin's materialism. Heredity with Butler was a spiritual force, working through a sort of unconscious memory. Birth and death are mere arbitrary landmarks ; identity is unbroken in the history of the individual; and memory is the controlling factor in the development of the race. Every organism works under the influence of memory, and, directly an organism is placed in surroundings of which it knows nothing, it must inevitably die. It is unnecessary to follow the divagations of Butler's system further ; its main issue with Darwinism was the issue between Chance and Purpose, or (to use Butler's own title) between Luck and Cunning. Darwin's evolutionary theory was, after all, founded upon Luck ; but Butler saw

Memory working through the processes of the physical world, moulding progress to its own pattern, and securing continuity throughout the life of the organism. In a phrase, Butler was the disciple of Free Will, and Darwin the disciple of Necessity.

But these are intricate questions, not even to be set forth in outline within the limits of a brief survey. The main thing about them is the certainty with which they display a transparently honest nature, struggling to deal faithfully with its generation. So honest indeed was the effort that Butler puzzled and annoyed his contemporaries by defying definition. England expects every man to bear his own label, and bursts into impatience with every talent which refuses to be pigeonholed. And Butler had no party to serve, and no recognisable programme to carry through. He refused to be solemn, even when he was serious : and the pedants declined to believe that any man, who had seriously conceived the apparently mad notion that the Odyssey was written by a woman, would be content to exploit it in language which always appeared to be laughing in its sleeve. But Butler's way was always the way of quiet laughter, and along that path he sought persistently for truth, and sought it clear-eyed and eager-hearted. He smiled as he went, but he was in deadly earnest all the time. He yearned to get down to essentials, and had little patience with fripperies and decorations. To him Character was the essence of life : Success a mere accident of fortune. And moving in a world where Success was regarded as the touchstone of merit, he found himself, for the most part, a pilgrim and a sojourner among his own people. Yet his very loneliness served his talent well; for by it he was rescued from the dangers of popularity, and the perils of success. His sincerity remained untainted, while the world went its way, heedless of his honest cynicism. But we have begun to learn a good deal since then; and there is more to learn yet, before we have done with our schooling. And among the schoolmasters to bring us to the light, not the least in authority and persuasiveness will be this indomitable seeker after truth, in whose pages we can read the record of the faults which we are called upon to amend, and read of them (to all the better profit) in that stimulating world of fancy, where Wit and Wisdom go blithely hand in hand.

THE CHARM OF STEVENSON

On the Trail of Stevenson. By Clayton Hamilton. With Illustrations by Walter Hale. London : Hodder and Stoughton

THEY are the few among authors—the few, the elect, the lovable—in whose honour the faithful make pilgrimages over land and sea ; and their " lovableness " is of the essence of the devotion. Mere greatness has no such lure ; for who cares to live with greatness ? The shrines of greatness are desolate and forbidding ; but the companionable quality of good-fellowship never forsakes a dead author, and men like Charles Lamb, Dickens, and Stevenson are secure against the taint of time, just because their spirits haunt the habitations of their life, till place and memory become so inextricably interwoven that the fancy can scarcely think of them apart. The lure may be very different ; it may be both personal and dramatic. The haunts of Charles Lamb, for instance, are chiefly loved because his own personality, mellow, fragrant, and humane, lingers around them ; but the multitudinous corners of " Dickens's England " owe their popularity to the superabundant vitality of his fictitious characters, a vitality so irresistible that Mr. Tupman's bedroom and Betsy Trotwood's cottage are solemnly displayed to visitors with as much interest as though Mr. Tupman and Miss Trotwood had really trodden their floors, and peeped through their lattice windows. Here, of course, lies the difference between the critical artist and the creative ; the one infects the world with his own personality, the other succeeds in making the creatures of his imagination a thousand times more actual than himself.

Now, the lure of Stevenson combines the two qualities, and gives him, and the places among which he moved, an intimate attraction which, if it is not actually unique, is at any rate very unusual. In art, if not in life, Stevenson was an inspired egotist ; he won his readers to an almost passionate devotion to his own personality. He absorbed the places he visited, and could not rest until by some ingenuity of interpretation he had identified them with himself. But he was also a novelist, and the scenes of his stories are real, and easily to be discovered. So that he has a double claim upon the places where he lived—a personal and an artistic claim ; and the more one appreciates the temperament of the author himself, the better will one enjoy the wonderful little pen-pictures in which he fixes upon the page the elusive characteristics of the places that he loved. And so Mr. Clayton Hamilton, in following the trail of Stevenson across two hemispheres, has a difficult, but a very fascinating task. That he has performed it with so much success proves him to be a critic and an interpreter of true quality and force.

The book comes from America, and has all the native American curiosity and persistency. The author has scamped nothing. He has visited even the remotest spots associated with R. L. S., and has exchanged confidences with all his principal surviving friends. The work could not be more thoroughly done ; but Mr. Hamilton has something more than industry and care to distinguish him. He has also taste. His record is penetrating, but it keeps invariably clear from the taint of impertinence ; the author's curiosity never leads him astray. Good judgment and a cultured style do honour to their theme, and enlighten it with the graces of sentiment and restraint. The most exclusive of the old Stevenson circle could hardly fail to appreciate and approve.

The first and most notable truth about the haunts of Stevenson is the fact that, in the accepted sense of the word, he never had a home at all. Stevenson was a wanderer from his birth, an absolute stranger to the homing spirit. Mr. Edmund Gosse has related how, while the rest of his contemporaries settled down and acquired the impedimenta of the householder, Stevenson was wont to laugh at their encumbrances, and despise their provinciality. He himself had no continuing city : he was an Ariel of the open field. But, if he can be pinned down to any tarrying-place, the imagination will always associate him most closely with that " grey metropolis of the winds," whose " beauty of natural locality, impressiveness of monumental grandeur, and richness of romantic atmosphere " kept calling his fancy back to the most congenial home he ever knew—the Edinburgh of his boyhood. Something in his own temperament seems peculiarly akin to that keen and questing city of dreams. He never forgot " the august air of the castle on its rock, nocturnal passages of lights and trees . . . the building up of the city on a misty day, house above house, spire above spire, until it was received into a sky of softly glowing clouds, and seemed to pass on and upward, by fresh grades and rises, city beyond city, a new Jerusalem, bodily scaling heaven." Edinburgh was undoubtedly his nearest approach to home, and with it went also his young memories of the Pentland Hills, which were later on to be enshrined in the pages of "St. Ives" and "Weir of Hermiston."

It is typically characteristic of Stevenson's invalid condition through life that, just as his brain was always most buoyant in bed, so his recollection was liveliest and most detailed in absence. It was from Hyères, after twenty years of separation from the garden of Colinton Manse, that he wrote with such eager accuracy the impressions of that enchanted pleasaunce of his childhood. It was in Vailima, after an even longer exile, that he set out his glowing inventory of the charms of Swanston Cottage, with its "air of a rambling, infinitesimal cathedral." And with these must be commemorated that ideal holiday refuge, Cramond on the Firth of Forth—"a little hamlet on a little river, embowered in woods, and looking forth over a great flat of quicksand to where a little islet stood planted in the sea." The tenderness of all these keen descriptions is one more proof that, if ever R. L. S. was at home, it was in Scotland.

In England certainly he was never at home; he could not appreciate the country, nor get upon easy terms with its inhabitants. Perhaps its stern conventionality chilled him; and the youth whom Mr. Gosse describes to us may well have seemed an exile in Piccadilly, in his " suit of blue sea-cloth, a black shirt, and a wisp of yellow carpet that did duty for a neck-tie." At any rate, his clearness of touch seems to fail him when he writes of England ; and though he made a home at Bournemouth, the choice was purely a question of his health. He never cared for the place, which he dismissed, not without justice, as " an uncharted wilderness of villas." But in France, freely embracing the nomad life which lay nearest to his heart, he was at least as happy as he could be. He felt well there, and he could enjoy life. He liked the people, and their pleasant, easy-going civilisation. The absence of restraint, the freedom, the romantic imagination of the country warmed his heart. His dreams went hunting back into the Middle Ages. He revelled in Avignon, where " the air was filled with sunset and the sound of bells " ; in Fontainebleau ; in Barbizon, and in all those sweet, shady villages, the memory of which dissolves itself into a mist of " lilies, and mills, and the foam and thunder of weirs." But, wherever he went, with his dreamy, observant eyes, he found himself in everything, and impressed his own personality upon his surroundings. As Mr. Hamilton says, he saw just as much as he needed to see for the purposes of his work, and what he needed to see was always overshadowed by the visionary domination of himself.

When we ask, however, what was the secret of that personality, praised by one of his best friends as " the most inspiriting, the most fascinating being that I have ever known," we find ourselves in a tangle of uncertainties. Mr. Gosse challenges the description of him as an egotist, protesting that there never was a truer altruist born among men than Stevenson. But it is possible to be intensely interested in the affairs of one's friends, and yet to be even more absorbed in one's own ; and whatever Stevenson may have been upon the beaten path of friendship, nobody who reads his books can doubt that his prevailing *literary* interest was himself. In Mr. Hamilton's happy phrase, he was " self-enjoying " ; and " a self-enjoying nature such as his takes possession of its own experience with a completeness that is without precedent in the habit of the average man." " The first quality," says Andrew Lang, " which strikes his reader is the buoyancy, the survival of the child in him." Putting these two estimates together, we have, perhaps, the true key to Stevenson's irresistible charm. The child survived, and triumphed in him ; and the naïve, unconscious egotism of childhood is always an imperishable delight to the rest of the older, greyer world.

In the last letter which he ever wrote, R. L. S. described himself as " a childless, rather bitter, very clear-eyed, blighted youth," and almost in the same context smiled at himself for having nothing in his " foolish, elderly head but love-stories." The two phrases supplement one another like broken utterances from a sincere confessional. Having no children of his own in whom to lose himself, Stevenson renewed his youth by continual reference to his memory, and the characters in his books are all facets of his own temperament. He is not a great creative artist, but his interpretation of moods and impulses is wonderfully sensitive, because it is almost always personal and reminiscent. He remained perennially a child, playing at being something other than he was, with all the freakish fancy of an imaginative infant. Even such prosaic spots as Charing Cross and Trafalgar Square became for him the centres of an Oriental romance ; such fantasy, as Andrew Lang said, is " like the work of a changeling." The same is true of his adventures among beach-combers and savages. It is all a magnificent game of make-believe. " The eternal child in him " beckons him from one exploit to another ; and all the while he holds his breath in elf-like and fantastical enjoyment.

It may be that his reputation has dimmed a little in the interval of twenty years ; at any rate the young men-of-letters no longer seem to sharpen their arrows upon the whetstone of his brilliant, many-coloured, occasionally laborious style. The essayists of the eighteenth century, upon whom he modelled himself, are too deliberate for the slap-dash methods of the hour ; and the Thackeray, with whom he qualified his Addison and Steele, is too meditative and, perhaps, too moralising for the latest taste. Yet Stevenson will never fall away from the company of the elect. The wistful, companionable charm of his personality is secure. He has the true secret at his heart. " The eternal child " in all of us remains the same from generation to generation. Everything is forgiven it, everything is conceded. The soul of youth is perpetually irresistible.

THE ART OF HENRY JAMES

HENRY JAMES. By Rebecca West. (Writers of the Day.) Nisbet.

TO distil the essence of the art of Henry James into a little volume of about 20,000 words is no light labour; and Miss Rebecca West must be congratulated upon the degree of success with which she has accomplished the undertaking. In several respects this is a book which its subject would have well approved. In a letter which lies before me now, addressed to the present writer some sixteen years ago, Henry James complained that the art of brief biography seemed very little understood in this country, and that short " Lives " had a way of wasting themselves in facts and anecdotes, instead of conveying a general and spiritual impression of what the subject was, and of what he stood for. Miss West, at any rate, has fallen into no such error. She deals very little with facts, and very freely with impressions; and she succeeds in giving a definite, clear, and attractive portrait of a very elusive and complex artistic personality.

Miss West, we say, deals sparingly with anecdotes, but there is one story upon which, with genuine insight, she builds her whole conception of Henry James's character and art. She recalls the fact that, when the American Civil War broke out, in Henry James's eighteenth year, he was incapacitated, by a sudden, severe accident, from all possibility of military service, while his brothers went plunging through the fiery experiences of the campaign which transformed the whole existence, and revolutionised all the standards, of the American people. And in that period of inevitable isolation, says Miss West, Henry James " worked out a scheme of existence, in which the one who stood aside, and felt rather than acted, acquired thereby a mystic value, a spiritual supremacy, which . . . would be rubbed off by participation in action." Here is a vivid flash of critical insight, revealing its subject in high relief. For Henry James, as an artist, was always a looker-on at life ; and it was just this analytical detachment of the looker-on which gave to his art its peculiar savour and intensity. The looker-on, we are all aware, sees more of the game than the player ; but he is also apt, if his temperament is at all sensitive, to suffer more in the excitement of anticipation than the player himself suffers in the hot intensity of action. In the same way the looker-on at life sees the pain and pathos of the moment, plumbs it to its depth, and then, by a sudden return upon himself, compares the present moment with the past, idealises his memory of calmer moods, and by glorifying what is not actual, adds an intensity of pathos to the actuality of the hour. And there, in a nutshell, is the method of Henry James. He is always a spectator of life, moralising its inequalities ; and his sensibility to the distress of the moment is so acute that his mind perpetually seeks relief in the recollection of circumstances happier and more tranquil. All such relief, of course, is illusory, for the pageant of life is an unending processional of pain. Yet, as the vision of actuality presses more and more upon the artist's consciousness, it becomes almost the only way of escape possible to a sympathy overburdened with the sorrows of the world.

This sort of "divine discontent" with his environment was, no doubt, first instilled into Henry James through the sense of being a citizen of two continents, with no continuing city in either. While still a boy he had travelled in Europe, and returned to America to find it a raw, experimental civilisation, struggling to build its ideals out of unpromising material. America was already much impressed by European standards, but still incapable of transplanting them into its own hard soil. And so, in the effort to appreciate one another, the two communities, bound by so many native ties of blood and association, were constantly brought into collision, and exposed to the disappointment of mutual misunderstanding. The pity of this state of things depressed our young novelist profoundly, and overshadowed a large group of his early stories. "Roderick Hudson," "The American," and "Daisy Miller," in particular, are saturated with these problems; and as a rule each of the new presentations takes the form of an implicit apologia for the American temperament. The novelist is half in love with both nations, but intuitive loyalty obliges him to make out the best case for his own. It is only by degrees that he emerges from a national novelist into the broader light of pure psychology.

Slowly but firmly, however, he developed his point of view. Starting from an intense sympathy with his own countrymen, he began to appreciate, as he studied them under the microscope, that there is something larger and more beneficent than nationality. The spirit of French literature began to pervade his work, and he became more and more detached ; more intimately, and at the same time more universally, a looker-on. Already in " Daisy Miller " he had lighted upon the situation which was always to make the most powerful appeal to his sympathies—the spectacle, that is, of unconscious innocence in the clutch of the suspicion and misinterpretation of conscious vice. And from that standpoint he elaborated by degrees his series of studies of " beauty and anguish, walking hand in hand the downward slope to death." Whether through renunciation, forgiveness, or resignation, his characters were continually brought face to face with the necessity of preferring another's interest to their own ; unselfishness and sacrifice were seen to be the essence of the pathos of life, and the essence also of its triumphant achievement.

And so Henry James became the foremost living exponent of the novel of analytic impressionism. The intellectual vigour and variety of his analysis seemed sometimes almost tantalisingly inexhaustible. But the method was always the same. It probed to the heart of a motive ; but revealed, not the realistic surroundings of an action, but the suggested mental processes which prompted it. Then it carried forward the same method to embrace the result of the action. The passive characters are studied in direct reference to the intellectual and moral impression which the action produces; almost every movement of the actor is exploited as a manifestation of a suppressed emotion. How elaborate the machinery could become, when "he" was wondering whether "she" could possibly think that "he" had conceived "her" capable of fancying, etc., every student of Henry James's later stories is painfully aware. But the fascination of following up the intricate play of minor emotions was generally irresistible, and the splendid, sustaining estimate of human nature, which underlay all the lace-work of motive and apprehension, was in itself a liberal spiritual education.

The world, he seemed to say, is full of sorrow and tribulation, but the soul of man justifies itself by its patience and endurance. Purity, innocence, the simple heart, are its only lasting possessions. They will inevitably be misunderstood; but even so they are abundantly worth while. For a man must be able to respect himself before he can be at peace with the world. And the sincerity of this belief was unceasingly evident in Henry James's own life; he lived, if ever man did so, in harmony with all he wrote. It is impossible to imagine him making any compromise with what he believed to be true, least of all because such a compromise was likely to be popularly acceptable. His picture of life was as near to the real thing as he could make it, and it was drawn with a fidelity which spared no pains to render every detail of motive and impression accurate and communicable. To all his brothers of the pen he was a shining example of true and honourable work. A more courteous, kindly gentleman (in the half-forgotten sense of the word) never stepped the earth. No man of his time was freer from the petty jealousies and misprisions which so often hinder and degrade the literary career He had a welcome for every kind of new movement in art and letters, provided only it was honest and sincere. There are very few of the younger generation of writers who have not had cause to be grateful for his encouragement and advice. He was one of the first to recognise the talent of Mr. Rudyard Kipling and of Hubert Crackanthorpe (talents indeed sufficiently diverse !), and during the last year or so of his life he gave conspicuous evidence that the work of nearly all the newer school of novelists had been with him the subject of scrupulous and appreciative attention. It is possible, as Miss West suggests, that his literary criticism was too warmhearted to be final : that he was always over-willing to be pleased. But that was a concession over which his contemporaries were not likely to cavil. It endeared him to his whole generation, and there were few men-of-letters of our time more universally and intimately beloved.

Finally, it is not likely to be forgotten that, by establishing the standards of a new form of fiction, Henry James bridged the gulf between the stalwart giants of the Victorian era and the eager, experimental spirit of the Georgians. When he began to write, the novel of incident, as a serious form of literature, had just about outlived its day ; there was nothing more to be done with it, and a new departure was essential. That departure, into the region of pure psychological analysis, Henry James effected, in the face of much discouragement, popular neglect, and even artistic misunderstanding. Yet, if we look around us to-day, we can see that it is his example which has inspired most of the brilliant younger men ; and his methods, however infinitely modified, which lie at the heart of their creation. He loved youth, and his love is crowned with the loyalty of youth. Whatever the younger men may say about some of the idols of their parents' adolescence, they have none of them anything but respect and admiration for the memory and the art of Henry James.

DIXON SCOTT'S CRITICISM

MEN OF LETTERS. By Dixon Scott. With an Introduction by Max Beerbohm. London: Hodder and Stoughton.

THE art of literary criticism is undoubtedly the most difficult of all the arts in which to establish a popular reputation. If Dixon Scott, the author of this very striking volume of essays, had been a novelist, a playwright, or even a poet, and had put forth work in any of these lines one half so good as the work that is here collected from various scattered sources, it is safe to say that he would have been well known and recognised wherever people interested in literature meet and talk. Yet, when he died, as Mr. Max Beerbohm says, very few even of those who are occupied with books and journalism were familiar with his name; and this collection of his critical writings will come as a surprise to many. It is true that he preferred a provincial audience to a metropolitan, and to some extent that may account for his being so little known in London. To secure anything like a popular name in town, it is no doubt necessary to mingle with one's fellow-men, to be seen abroad in what is called (often very falsely) "literary society," and to be commended over tea-tables, by those omniscient and garrulous women who have always so much to say about the declining circulation of Miss Gusher, or the advancing royalties of Mr. Boom.

But the difference between a provincial and a metropolitan outlet is not enough to explain the general ignorance of Dixon Scott's challenging criticism. Besides, he did signed work, and much of it his best, in London periodicals as well. The fact is, of course, that the average man is not interested in criticism at all, and that the " literary women," who bubble over the tea-cups, can only appreciate two kinds of notices—the frankly and shamelessly flattering, on the one hand, and the flabbily platitudinous upon the other. Now, Dixon Scott dealt neither in flattery, nor in platitude. He loved the art of the writer, and he had nothing to say about it but what he believed to be the truth. To attain to that truth, and to keep his vision clear, he chose to live in the provinces, out of the reach of coteries and cliques. He believed (what many will doubt) that the atmosphere of a provincial town is more favourable to freedom of judgment and clarity of insight than the atmosphere of London. He had opportunities of academic distinction and comparative ease, but he relinquished them in order to live among the books he loved, and to secure himself the leisure in which to write about them worthily of his devotion. Then came the war ; and like so many other young men of a high spiritual conscience, he volunteered for service. Within three weeks of landing in Gallipoli he died of dysentery, on board a hospital ship. Before he enlisted, he had been engaged in collecting some of his essays into a book, and had begun expanding and rewriting them for the purpose. He recognised that the sharp, vigorous attack of a newspaper article needed the mellowing influence of proportion and perspective before it could become a finished essay. Some of the papers here printed had received that perfecting touch at his own hands ; others, now collected by the pious care of a friend, lack, and lack conspicuously, that saving benefit. The difference in the quality of the workmanship is very marked, but even in the least important of the papers the reader will recognise abundant traces of an original, eager, and penetrating mind, tremendously interested in its task, and avid for truth. Here, he will say, is the brain of a *man* at work on literature, tackling it in manly fashion, and determined to tear the heart out of it at any cost. And indeed so virile a temperament is no common possession in the modern literary life.

The whole standard of virility in criticism has, of course, changed enormously in the country during the last twenty years. Some sort of virility must, for example, be conceded to that school of criticism which went out with Churton Collins ; the school that flung about such phrases as " Will it be credited ? " and " Is it to be believed ? " and always started (and often ended) its survey of the book reviewed by testing all the dates with a biographical dictionary, and making a tremendous display of indignation over any incorrect numeral it could ferret out. With all such pedantic violence Dixon Scott had simply nothing in common. He set out not to destroy, but to make alive ; not to dissect, but to interpret. With him, as with every modern critic worth considering, literature was a thing not of facts and dates, but of ideas and life. Life and literature were found to be inextricably interwoven, and the true function of the critic was conceived as a duty of interpretation, revealing the qualities of literature in its direct relation to life. And since life reveals itself in a different aspect to every spiritual adventurer, it followed of necessity that the interpretation must needs be coloured, and in its more subtle aspects deeply coloured, by the personality of the interpreter. Truth was indeed its quest, but it could only be the truth apprehended by the individual seer. And so once more criticism becomes the adventure of a soul among masterpieces, and the more valuable, the greater and the more provocative the adventure.

Provocative is, indeed, the very word to describe Dixon Scott's criticism. In the essays here collected, at any rate, he attacks themes already rather threadbare ; and the natural temptation is to adopt a point of view that shall be startling at the outset. The reader will therefore find himself confronted with judgments, alike upon matters of fact and of opinion, which will probably arouse an irresistible impulse to retort. We read, for instance, that Browning never had so many, or such hearty and lusty admirers as in the year of his centenary : a statement which any bookseller or librarian could refute with statistics. Also that Browning's air of dangerous abstruseness is largely due to a kind of domestic economy, which used the material nearest to his hand. In a word, that Browning is a homely poet, analysing the emotions of the ordinary man—a truly Chestertonian obiter dictum. Or again, of Mr. Bernard Shaw, we are told that he is by nature eager, idealistic, impulsive, romantic, and that he took upon himself "as his deepest duty" the thankless task of challenge and contempt. If Dixon Scott had lived to read some of the utterances of Mr. Shaw during the last few years, he would almost certainly have felt compelled to modify this opinion. Equally paradoxical is the suggestion that Mr. Rudyard Kipling assumed the literary cocksureness and swagger of his youth as a kindly covert for his native shyness. No one who is familiar with the progress of Mr. Kipling's career could possibly swallow this judgment with equanimity. It is impossible to resist the conviction that Dixon Scott, having to write about authors who had already been sufficiently over-written, was intuitively driven to adopt an original and unexpected standpoint, if he was to find anything worth saying to say. And so he yielded to the easy temptation to invent a theory, and then to select and group his examples in support of it.

The result, of course, is that he is often more provocative than reasonable ; but it is an open question whether his work is not all the more refreshing on that account. It is delightfully stimulating to share the company of a man who is not afraid of holding views, even if those views are apt to prove wayward and intractable. The plain answer to the fact that Browning is " the poet for plain people " is the common experience that plain people have never been able to tolerate him. Turn a member of the Stock Exchange on to " Fifine at the Fair," and test it for yourself.

But out of these frequently untenable hypotheses there issues an infinite number of brilliant side-lights, by whose intermittent flashes we gradually get the revelation of a true and impressive portrait.

Perhaps the best of all the essays is that upon Sir James Barrie, whose whimsical temper is exactly suited to the critic's whimsical treatment. But in many other cases he is scarcely less happy in touching the essentials of the artist's mind, and in particular of his method. For it is with questions of method that Dixon Scott is peculiarly at home. Never in our own generation has there been so suggestive a critic of style. He loves to take a writer's sentences, and pull them to pieces, testing the tricks and cadences by which he achieves his effects. Here again his insatiable curiosity often leads him into exaggeration. He is never far removed from the risk of trying to read into a man's style more than it really contains. He will take a sentence like the following—" Just where the stone tooth rose out of the snow the snow swelled out, gum-like, a little," and pronounce it to be a series of dactyls ! It is certainly very ugly prose, but a worse collection of " dactyls " was never gathered together, even in the English tongue. There is indeed only one passable dactyl in the whole phrase. But, on the other hand, his analysis of Mr. Kipling's method is by far the best piece of criticism to which the author of " Kim " has ever been subjected. He finds the secret of his work in that passion for order and obedience, which is proclaimed *ore rotundo* in the dedication of " Stalky and Co.," and in the whole philosophy of " Macandrew's

Hymn." This devotion to machine-like regularity is shown to pervade every sentence which Mr. Kipling writes, irradiating his workmanship with a sense of design, mechanical, almost metallic, "stamping insubstantial dream-stuff into shapes as clear-cut and decisive as newly-milled and minted metal discs." That is a brilliant phrase, illuminating the Kipling manner in a lightning-flash.

Equally clever is his swift intuition of the real effect of Mr. Wells, when his cold, dictatorial "knuckle-rapping" method is suddenly invaded by a tide of true feeling, and human nature bursts the barriers of machinery. Of one of Mr. Wells's characters the critic says: "He has a brain like a lamp, and a body of steel, and a heart bubbling with poetry and joy." The criticism might with perfect justice be switched on to Mr. Wells himself, with whom, until the bubbling heart breaks free, the best of the artist never emerges. There is an equally incisive summary of Mr. Arnold Bennett, whose provincial love of life has never been beaten out of him by the grinding traffic of the Strand, and who revels in an aggressively male definiteness, which distrusts suggestion, and is impervious to a hint. "His very visions," he says, "are passed on to us as observations." Was the historian of the "Five Towns" ever so comprehensively epitomised?

There is much more to say of Dixon Scott; for, as Mr. Beerbohm protests, in his searching introduction, directly you begin to quote from him, you are overwhelmed with a desire to go on. He provokes argument, as every good critic must ; and to every second judgment he will inevitably appear to be pressing too assiduously in one direction, and to be making his points at the cost of fact and evidence. Yet, after all, what are facts, and what is evidence ? Every counsel of capacity twists the facts to his own purposes, and turns the evidence inside out. There are no such things as facts apart from the ideas which invest them with being ; and the one thing we ask of criticism is that it should be permeated with ideas, and out of its fiery flow should stir the current of our own slower and more obstinate intuition. And in that beneficent purpose the work of Dixon Scott never for one moment fails.

Mr. ARTHUR SYMONS'S CRITICISM

Figures of Several Centuries. By Arthur Symons. London: Constable.

IT is no new thing that a true poet should also be a good critic; and Mr. Arthur Symons stands in the direct succession of a dynasty that glitters with brilliant names. It may indeed be a doubtful point whether he best realises his faculties as a creator or as a critic; but at any rate there can be no question that his criticism will rank among the most penetrating and illuminative of our time. He possesses in a high degree the cardinal virtues of the critic; his judgment is at once well-balanced and receptive. The critic, of course, must always interpret by bringing his own sympathy and temperament to bear upon the temperament of his subject; it is out of the clash of personalities that interpretation must proceed. But if the critic's temperament is unbalanced, wayward, capricious, his picture will have the same defects; and the conspicuous vice of so much modern criticism is that, in its effort to revolt against platitude, it breaks out into the feverish excesses of forced originality. The newest school of criticism indeed is so anxious to prove its own individuality that it quarrels with established methods simply for the sake of quarrelling. Whatever is old, or even mellow, becomes contemptible; and it is forgotten that truisms have grown hackneyed merely by reason of their incontestable truth. Criticism nowadays is in danger from self-conceit. There is plenty of assertion, but very little submission; and, unless the critic submits himself to his subject, like a *dévot* to his faith, he will never find his way to the heart of the thing he tries to interpret.

Mr. Arthur Symons, by contrast, is the perfect type of the sympathetic, receptive critic. You do not need to agree with him every time, in order to appreciate that he approaches every subject in a mood of eager humility, that seeks to interpret through enlightenment. He does not flourish his own personality under his subject's eyes, but sets himself to learn before he begins to proclaim. Like all the best of his kind, he employs a sensitive style which keeps pace with his judgment. It avoids all violence; its balance and proportion are perfect; it is the scholar's prose, touched to colour by the poet's warm-hearted appreciation. It might, perhaps, be objected that the poet is, if anything, too much alive in Mr. Symons for his judgment to keep an impeccable balance. Beauty, it is true, is of the essence of his quest; and, though he has always been an advocate of realism, he parts company with the realist directly ugliness intrudes upon his work. He has little taste for Walt Whitman, and the dramatic actuality of Ibsen disturbs his taste. He does not always appreciate, in short, that an ugly emotion can only be displayed in an ugly phrase. This may be a limitation, but nowadays a little more of such limitation would be a wholesome quality in criticism. There is a great deal too much praise of the sheerly ugly and the forcibly vehement, and far too little sense of that elusive spirit of beauty without which no work of art was ever brought to perfection.

But it must not be imagined that Mr. Symons extols workmanship at the expense of intellect ; his passion for intellect in literature is the guiding principle of his judgment, as indeed his very choice of subjects indicates. The writer who appeals to him is always the writer who displays character in art, and the critic is keen to show how indissolubly character and art are intermingled in all essential literature. Perhaps the most suggestive of all the essays in the present volume is that upon John Donne, where the interaction of character and art is traced with intimate skill and insight. Donne's life is displayed in three stages of self-realisation. In youth he was a soldier, lover, and poet, plunging without restraint into all the pleasures and lures of life. This was his first stage. Then, in middle age, he became a lawyer and theologian, eager and almost unscrupulous in the pursuit of knowledge and advancement. Finally, in old age, he sank into the peace of religious contemplation, finding rest for the restless in meditation upon divinity, and a satisfying occupation as ambassador of God. Donne's art, in every stage, moved harmoniously with his life. He began, in his salad days, with a fervent realism of which perhaps he was the first example in English lyric poetry :

For God's sake, hold your tongue, and let me love,

he cries ; and again :

Nature's lay idiot, I taught thee to love.

When his passion is spurned, he avenges it in an outburst of biting invective. He suffers love like a disease, is half woman in his sensuous abandonment, and more than half woman in his marvellous intuition into feminine moods and vicissitudes of passion. No less sincerely, when he changes his loyalty, and transfers his passion from woman to God, he carries with him the same mental emotion, the same bitter curiosity about the metaphysical analysis of the soul. His naked heart is shown to God with an astounding sincerity of revelation. The one burning aim of his art is to be sincere, to deal honestly with himself in the confessional. His intellect is perpetually tearing down the veils of shame and pretence, and baring passion, human and divine, to the judgment of God and man.

Sincerity in life and art is the one quality that Mr. Symons demands of his literary idols ; and there is this affinity, bridging the long years, between Donne and Meredith (of whom he writes with equal certainty and force) that both worked in poetry, as it were, with the intellect for spade, and both threw up, in the course of their labours, a large quantity of rough and unshaped material. More than this, the sincerity of both laid its benignant hand upon the worker, so that he achieved beauty, as it were, by accident. Like Donne, Meredith reasons in verse ; but his reasoning emerges rather through imagery and imagination than by any direct and conscious metaphysical process. Meredith sees the world in terms of pictorial art, and transfigures the material world with the interpretation of the immaterial. Energy burns in his veins, burns so fiercely as to shrivel up the very grace and clarity of expression. But the genius is there, smouldering in a deathless fire, and breaking out anew into a clearer light, as the judgment recovers from the first shock of the vehement conflagration.

These may serve as samples of Mr. Symons's characteristic estimate of the artistic temperament, but his critical skill is far from being confined to the study of character alone. Being a poet himself, he is naturally sensitive about the technicalities of the art, and much of the best criticism in the volume is concerned with workmanship and prosody. He does not, like Dixon Scott, analyse the method of his subject, pull it to pieces like machinery, and show how the thing is done. His interest is that of the interpreter rather than of the mechanician ; he deals with the mass, and not with the details. And, after all, this is the subtler art. To interpret style in a phrase is one of the most difficult tasks that lies before the critic. Mr. Symons, however, has the art at his finger-tips. Take this, of Swinburne :

> His music has never the sudden bird's flight, the thrill, pause, and unaccountable ecstasy of the very finest lyrics of Blake or of Coleridge ; one never wholly forgets the artist in the utterance. But where he is incomparable is in an "arduous fulness" of intricate harmony, around which the waves of melody flow, foam and scatter like the waves of the sea about a rock. No poet has ever loved or praised the sea as Swinburne has loved and praised it ; and to no poet has it been given to create music with words in so literal an analogy with the inflexible and vital rhythmical science of the sea.

It is doubtful whether Swinburne's style was ever more concisely crystallised into a paragraph: only a poet could so embody the principles of a poet's art in imagery and suggestion. And here, again, of the author of "Marius the Epicurean":

In the work of Pater, thought moves to music, and does all its hard work as if in play. And Pater seems to listen for his thought, and to overhear it, as the poet overhears his song in the air. It is like music, and has something of the character of poetry, yet, above all, it is precise, individual, thought filtered through a temperament, and it comes to us as it does because the style which clothes and fits it is a style in which, to use some of his own words, "the writer succeeds in saying what he *wills*."

It might conceivably be objected that there is a touch of preciosity in this last description; but it must be remembered that Pater himself was a master of the "precious" touch, and like all our critic's estimates, the phrase borrows its colour —sympathetically—from its theme. To express the judgment in terms congenial to the subject is one of the surest qualities of receptive and sympathetic criticism.

Standards are shifting rapidly nowadays: and it is not impossible that Mr. Symons is already relegated, by the newest creative movement in poetry, to the ranks of a generation whose verdicts are superseded and out of date. If so, all the worse for the taste of those who are contented to disregard him. He himself has always been sensitively alert to new sensations, so alert indeed, that it seems a strange reversal of fortune that his own work should be subjected to the common fate. In his heyday he was the most modern of the moderns. Although he is not altogether heartwhole in his praise of Ibsen, he belongs to that generation who caught fire from the independence and revolt of Ibsen's social dramas, and talked bravely, with Hedda Gabler about the courage of living one's own life, and the splendour of irresponsibility. The young ambition of that period was for the realisation of self—to break away from convention : "To hedge about what is one's own, and keep it free and clean from everything outside that has no connection with it." Sincerity was its watchword ; and sincerity in outlook and in art is the one thing for which Mr. Symons's criticism indefatigably clamours. He can honour sincerity in the keen material satire of Ibsen no less than in the mystical vision of Coventry Patmore. He even honours it so much as to pardon for its sake the scarcely pardonable foible of conceit : and when Patmore glows with a protecting sense of his own poetic pre-eminence, Mr. Symons finds his arrogance "better, because franker, than the more customary pride that apes humility." And this sincerity, which he invites from others, he was always the first to offer in his own person. No man among his contemporaries is freer from the petty pretences of the literary life ; no man has been more decently honest about the primitive impulses of body and soul, and all that confused turmoil of moods, emotions, and first principles, out of which the permanent character of man slowly emerges into individuality. He is an honest critic, with open eyes, and a true student of life, with an open heart. His work will hold its own by the very virtue of that native sincerity without which all the ingenuity and cleverness of the artist is as dust before the wind of Time.

Mr. JOHN FREEMAN'S CRITICISM

The Moderns. By John Freeman. London: Robert Scott.

THE very young enthusiast who rushes to this volume, expecting to find all his newest gods enthroned and haloed, will be disappointed by its muster-roll; but he is the only person who *will* be disappointed by an uncommonly vivacious, tonic, and stimulating book. Mr. Freeman's "Moderns," it is true, are already the moderns of the middle distance. Three of them are dead, and none of the living is less than fifty years old; the newest and most revolutionary movement in literature is absolutely unmentioned in these vigorous pages. Nevertheless, the title is justified; for the men of whom Mr. Freeman writes are, many of them, the men who set going that modern movement which has now inevitably escaped out of their control, by ways that they could scarcely have foreseen. They are the men who first found voice for the prevailing restlessness with social and intellectual conditions, the itching dissatisfaction with the hindrances to life, and the eager aspiration towards some recompense withheld, yet not inaccessible, which combine in that persistent temperament so characteristic of our own modernity. And in tracing the line back to the origins of the present discontent, Mr. Freeman is right in concentrating his attention upon such writers as Henry James, Mr. H. G. Wells, Mr. Thomas Hardy and Mr. Joseph Conrad—all of whom in their different fashions have set themselves to probe the unrest of their generation, and to interpret it both to its own time and to those that come after.

There are two main classes of literary criticism—the analytic and the interpretative ; and Mr. Freeman's method may be said to incline rather towards the first of these. For, while the interpretative critic seeks chiefly to explain what an author set out to do, the analyst goes further, and questions the right and wrong of his author's standpoint ; and there is any amount of good, sound judgment and vivid challenge in Mr. Freeman's studies. He is refreshingly alert, agile, and combative. His admiration for his subject never steps over the border-line of idolatry ; his critical faculty is never permitted to repose. The result of his investigation, even where it most urgently provokes reply, is not for a moment otiose or negligible. He understands the time, and the spirit of the time. He places each of his heroes in reasonable relation with his age, and does so with an ingenuity that keeps the reader's intellect perpetually upon the move. Altogether, he has produced a thoroughly stimulating volume, wide in sympathy, and quick in insight.

We have noted that the pervading characteristics of modernity are dissatisfaction and revolt; and Mr. Freeman begins his study, cleverly enough, with an author who has not lacked the wit to echo the dissatisfaction, without possessing sufficient mental ballast to be able to suggest a way of escape from prevailing disadvantages. Mr. Freeman is, no doubt, right in saying that Mr. Bernard Shaw commenced dramatic authorship with a sincere desire to turn the theatre into something other than a shop of frivolity and sensuality; the mischief was that he had not himself enough human sympathy and heart to create real characters or to contrive a genuine situation. His own egoism broods over all his work; his characters are mere puppets employed to express their inventor's ideas. The trail of the galanty-show disfigures his theatre; and he is revealed, in Mr. Freeman's searching phrase, as a "comic playwright who is not a poet." The poet's touch—the true, creative touch of sympathy—is just what he always lacks. His lay-figures are "galvanically active"; they have movement, but they do not live. They are jerked about on strings in an atmosphere of stifling inhumanity. The pleasure which an audience derives from their evolutions is not far separated from the pleasure with which a music-hall crowd watches the set-to of a couple of knockabouts. The method is almost precisely the same; what the two Macs used to do with walking-sticks Mr. Shaw's characters do with words. The root of the whole matter is that the plays have no natural origin, but are merely cleverly-tinkered illustrations of ideas.

We advance a good deal nearer Nature, when we pass from Mr. Shaw to Mr. H. G. Wells. In a really brilliant essay in contrast Mr. Freeman sets the two old Fabians over against one another as the negative and positive products of improvisation. Mr. Shaw is the negative: Mr. Wells the positive. Mr. Shaw freezes and destroys; Mr. Wells warms and constructs. The prompting spirit of Mr. Wells's art is curiosity—the desire to understand. And then, when he understands evil, he burns to get rid of it. He is first thirsty for experience, and then eager to readjust conditions. His curiosity has bred in him the scientific trick of mind, together with the equally scientific passion for results. He is perpetually experimenting. He began his experiments with scientific romances, and passed thence to sociological studies. But, whatever his theme, the desire to get to the truth has been paramount; and to get to it, in order to suggest a more excellent way out of his own. Mr. Freeman places "Love and Mr. Lewisham" lower in the scale of Mr. Wells's works than the present writer would; and indeed Mr. Wells himself is absolutely right when he declares it to be one of the most carefully balanced of his books. But it is more than that. It is also one of his most winning books; and, though Mr. Freeman says that "few writers have charmed so skilfully as Mr. Wells," it is surely nearer the mark to admit that "charm" is a quality that is apt to desert these elaborately analytic studies of the modern mood. In his earlier novels Mr. Wells was often visited by the fairy godmother Charm; but as he grew more ambitious, the "social welter and perplexity," which he toils so hard to reflect, has more and more drowned out the grace of sympathy and the pure narrative gift. His art as a novelist has declined as his scope widened. His intellect, extraordinarily receptive and eruptive, has been changed into a whirlpool of contemporary impressions : he does not pause to separate the materials : his story becomes one seething cauldron of social and intellectual unrest. As Mr. Freeman puts it in a nutshell : he tends to produce " much activity but little power, haste without advance, curiosity without reflectiveness." He is for ever " scratching a worn road, with his back to the sun " ; voluminously explanatory, but not conspicuously advancing.

With Mr. Thomas Hardy, however, we arrive at a more stable and confident acceptance of the burden of modern doubt and restlessness. In him the feverishness of experiment is supplanted by a grave, almost sombre, philosophical view of life. Mr. Hardy goes straight to Nature, and learns from her. He is not afraid to face fundamental facts of temperament and character ; but he can only be called a pessimist by those who deliberately shut their eyes to the truth. And the special truth which Nature discloses to his investigation is the truth of its own cruelty. As Mr. Freeman puts it, there appears in Nature a sort of inevitable " untowardness," which tortures human relations, forbids happiness, and deals out penalty and punishment with the careless hand of injustice. Life is grim, sinister, malign ; and the more the heart sympathises with the height of human ambition, the more bitter does that malignity appear. Mr. Freeman reveals his critical grasp to the fullest advantage in his analysis of " Tess " ; and it would not perhaps be an exaggeration to say that no one has written more acutely upon this particular theme. " Does not Mr. Hardy," he asks, " load the dice against Tess ? " It is well said ; and it is indeed the most vulnerable trait in Mr. Hardy's chill sincerity that he cannot invariably resist the temptation to " load the dice," and to torture his characters beyond the limits of divine justice, or even of human proportion. The ironic spirit presides over his creation, and leads him over and over again into the trackless quagmire of dismay. He is a philosopher who has lost his way. He can show us life as it is, but he has no antidote to offer to the bitter revelation of the worst.

Perhaps, however, the provision of that antidote is the function rather of poetry than of fiction ; and it must not be overlooked that Mr. Freeman crowns his study of modernity by reference to the final sanction of the poet's art. His choice in poetry is austere ; with Coventry Patmore, Francis Thompson, and Mr. Robert Bridges as his chosen examples, he cannot be said to take the easy path. It is a path, nevertheless, which rounds off the quest with a resting-place. We look for some amulet against the insidious poison of modern discontent, and Patmore offers us the universal antidote to the suffering of the world, the only sure beacon in the night, —Love. Passion, as our critic remarks, is within the reach of most poets ; and illicit love is the favourite theme of many. But Patmore took the simplest and most sedate manifestation of Love, and irradiated it with high symbolism and divine significance. The primitive impulse of sex is sanctified by the supreme inspiration of Love, from which all good things spring, and to which all that is good must return at last, like falling water to the fountain. And in Patmore, as in the other two poets selected, a high theme is found to demand high treatment, so that the art of poetry is pursued with enthusiasm along the rugged road to technical perfection. In the work of the present Poet Laureate the gospel of Love is manifested in human emotions, transfigured by an almost superhuman ecstasy of spiritual submission : in Francis Thompson it issues in devotional fervour, wrestling with the Unseen, and demanding its blessing before the hour of contact passes. But all three agree in solving material problems in the light of immaterial ideals. They offer to the temporal troubles of the modern world the age-old solace of eternal Love: "tendentesque manus ripae ulterioris amore," they wait for the fruition of their peace in a state of intellectual quiescence, which is independent of the gifts, even as it is triumphant over the privations, of our struggling, depressed, but still indomitable humanity.

Mr. JOSEPH CONRAD AND THE DISCIPLINE OF FEAR

The Shadow Line. By Joseph Conrad. London: Dent.

AMONG the few living novelists whose reputation with their contemporaries appears to be absolutely assured, not more than two or three are so firmly established as Mr. Joseph Conrad. There seems to be no doubt about him ; his praise is in all schools of fiction ; the Old Guard and the New Regiment combine to do him honour. And this unanimity is, perhaps, the more impressive because Mr. Conrad makes no concession to tradition, and at the same time does nothing to conciliate the new rebellion. His novels have little of the method and construction of the accepted classics, nor do they permit themselves the leisurely panorama of detail which is fast taking the place of story-telling in the practice of the young. They triumph almost entirely by atmosphere, an atmosphere created by the sense of an inevitable spiritual conflict through which alone the soul of a man can realise its own capacity. Time after time the same problem is set upon the stage. Humanity is represented in opposition to the forces of Nature, and Nature itself is furnished with the weapons of Destiny. It is man's recurrent task to build up bulwarks against the incursion of Nature ; over and over again he watches these defences overborne ; but it is the man who endures to the end who alone achieves his manhood. To preserve that endurance he must be perpetually alert and vigorous ; it is a conflict of life and death, with brute force ranged on the one side, and on the other the tenuous defence of the human soul. But man's courage is equal to the ordeal, if only it be disciplined by experience, and hardened by a certain stern humility.

In some form or other this conflict is reflected in almost all Mr. Conrad's books, and the vogue which he has attained seems to suggest that the taste of novel-readers generally has grown much subtler and more serious, during the twenty years or so in which Mr. Conrad has been building up his public. For not only is the intellect always at work in his books, it is also urgently at work upon emotions and hesitations of the spirit which lie below the surface. In particular, Mr. Conrad evinces an absorbing interest in the mental processes of fear. One of the most perilous weapons which Nature can employ against the soul of man is the weapon of Fear ; it is the bane of the savage, and at the same time the germ of all his religious impulses. The cloud thunders ; and the savage, falling on his knees, worships the voice of a hidden god. Nor does the mystery vanish with the growth of civilisation. Many grown-up children in all ages, however well fortified with knowledge and faith, remain to their dying day inveterately frightened of the dark. And in this latest story (slight in fabric, but wonderfully complex and haunting in elaboration) Mr. Conrad advances the problem of Fear one step further : he takes it out of the region of the natural into the vague borders of the supernatural. And he does so once more through the medium of his favourite element, the sea.

Mr. Conrad has the spirit of the sea in his veins, and he knows it best perhaps in its most sinister moods. He has long since revealed the sea to us as something very like a living, brooding, dominating creature, moulding its children to its will, breaking them on the cruel wheel of its storm. That is the natural aspect of the sea, as a thing of terror, a dragon (as it were) in the way of the knight-errant, working out the salvation of his soul. And now he adds to the atmosphere of natural fear a supernatural element, mingling itself with the force of Nature, intertwining emotion with emotion, until it becomes almost impossible to say whether Nature is producing the supernatural atmosphere by natural means, or whether the supernatural power has for the moment seized upon Nature, overcome its processes, and bent its manifestations to its will. The shadow line is passed and repassed with bewildering intricacy ; and the victims, labouring in the darkness, are brought to the very gate of despair, in their impotence to fight the prevailing horror that engulfs them.

This is one aspect of the shadow line, but there is yet another which gives its distinguishing interpretation to the tale. In every man's life there comes a dividing period when youth, with its mist of indecision, emerges into manhood ; when purpose hardens, illusion fades away, and the road before the traveller grows clear. And the man who passes that line in safety is half-way towards his goal ; it is a critical point,—one, perhaps, of many,—but yet deadly critical. When it is past, the youth has become a man. And it is upon the border of this shadow line that Mr. Conrad sets the protagonist of this new, unnerving conflict between the spiritual will and the supernatural obsession. His hero is a young officer in the mercantile marine, who suddenly, under the languorous influence of an Eastern port, throws up his job, weary of the sea, and yet altogether ignorant of what he is to do next. It is a rash access of dissatisfaction, boredom, " green-sickness," familiar to all who know the ways of youth ; and, unless it is speedily countered by a contesting purpose, it is likely to head straight for disaster. Mr. Conrad's seaman is fortunate in being delivered from it by a wayward beneficence of chance. He has never commanded a vessel, and to do so is the native ambition of every son of the sea. Suddenly, as he kicks his heels in the officers' club of the Eastern port, there comes an offer to him, to pick up a command at once. A master of a British ship has died at Bangkok, and the Consul-General has cabled to the harbour-master for a competent man to be sent out to take command. It is the chance of a lifetime. The young man shakes off his lethargy, and is prepared to start without a night's delay. And from the moment he accepts the post, the thin, indefinable atmosphere of mystery begins to gather about his steps.

Mr. Conrad shares with Henry James the subtle

gift of conveying an atmosphere of mental and physical discomfort without the employment of any visible machinery of horror. Compared with the lurid methods, say, of Bulwer Lytton, this delicate playing upon the nerves is like the swift sleight of hand of a modern conjuror, contrasted with the double-bottomed boxes and heavily-tinkered paraphernalia of the stage wizard of forty years ago. It is difficult, in turning over the pages again, to fix upon any precise passage in the story as marking the moment, when the reader becomes aware that there is something uncanny and uncomfortable going on. The impression forms itself in vague and shadowy outline, imperceptible in its deepening, until at last the whole air is full of menace. The ship looks comely enough, when her new captain first sees her in the morning light, " a creature of high speed, an Arab steed in a string of cart-horses." When he steps on board her, all is trim and shining; the brasses gleam; the sunlight plays upon a hundred flashing points. Yet in the very inheritance of his proud possession there flits a sudden cloud across the brain. Something is wrong: the air of the ship is heavy with suggestion: and the secret suddenly takes form in the watching, suffering, malignant eyes of the chief mate. The truth is that the ship is haunted, for those who have sailed on her before, by the spirit of the dead captain, who lies, many fathoms below the oily sea, in 8º 20′ of latitude, and who, before he died, cursed his ship, and all that were on her, with the dying prayer that she might never come into port.

Slowly, insidiously, with the gliding motion

of a snake, the terror of this dead man's influence closes round the vessel. They get her out beyond the bar, and then the hot calm settles down upon her, and nothing will move her. The sea conspires with the dead : Nature and the supernatural join in an unholy compact : disease attacks the crew, and the quinine bottles in the medicine chest are found to be full of rubbish. There is no means of combating the mortal sickness, and the chief mate, who was responsible for his captain's burial, begins to go mad under the feverish conviction that, if one of the men dies, " the old man " will have got above them, and they will all be damned of body and soul.

Against this crescent terror there is opposed only the will of the new captain, who, having had no experience of the earlier horror, is immune from its withering power. The problem of the conflict centres here. Will the will of man be strong enough to live down the unclean influence ? Destiny and human courage are at odds, and the sole support of the young captain in his battle with fate is a cheery, loyal steward, himself the victim of heart disease, who refuses to yield to the surrounding terror, and helps his skipper to keep going in the face of overwhelming obstacles. The skill with which the spectral grip of the dead man is kept hovering over the yard-arms of the fated vessel is simply inimitable. The only thing in modern fiction to be compared with it is the ghostly taint of the degenerate servant in Henry James's " Turn of the Screw." And all the while the sea co-operates with the dead, whose secret it has inherited, to torture the imagination of the living. The panorama of sweltering day and night is pictured in a series of wonderful cameos from Nature. By day the unchanging prospect is an overpowering burden.

Mysterious currents drifted us here and there, with a stealthy power made manifest by the changing vistas of the islands fringing the east shore of the Gulf. And there were winds too, fitful and deceitful. They raised hopes only to dash them into the bitterest disappointment, promises of advance ending in lost ground, expiring in sighs, dying into dumb stillness in which the currents had it all their own way—their own inimical way.

At night the black solitude closes round like a shroud :

The only spot of light in the ship at night was that of the compass-lamps, lighting up the faces of the succeeding helmsmen ; for the rest we were lost in the darkness, I walking the poop and the men lying about the decks. They were all so reduced by sickness that no watches could be kept. Those who were able to walk remained all the time on duty, lying about in the shadows of the main deck, till my voice raised for an order would bring them to their enfeebled feet, a tottering little group, moving patiently about the ship, with hardly a murmur, a whisper amongst them all.

The will of the dead man—that his ship shall never pass the spot where he lies in his vast and wandering grave—holds heaven and ocean in a deathly quiescence, until a night comes, when the blackness is blacker than the bottomless pit, and all Nature seems waiting breathless for the final liberation of these prisoners of the soul. Then, without warning, the deluge breaks :

> Suddenly—how am I to convey it ? Well, suddenly the darkness turned into water. This is the only suitable figure. A heavy shower, a downpour, comes along, making a noise. You hear its approach on the sea, in the air too, I verily believe. But this was different. With no preliminary whisper or rustle, without a splash, and even without the ghost of impact, I became instantaneously soaked to the skin.

The storm had come at last, the wind had risen, the ropes creaked in the pulleys, the sails began to feel the breeze. The spirit of fear was beaten, and the vessel was moving to the nearest port, with all her sick at death's door, but with all of them still alive. It was indeed a return upon their tracks ; they had not yet crossed the shadow-line where the dead captain lay. Before that could be done the ship must have another crew, free from the influence of fear. But for the time the present crew are delivered from their spiritual bondage. " The old man " could do them no more wrong now.

It is Mr. Conrad's favourite conflict once more,—the victory of man's courage over the powers of evil. But by the time the victory has been won, the shadow line between youth and maturity is passed. The young captain comes out of the ordeal an altered man. He says that he feels " old," but he is not really old. The truth is simply that he is no longer young. Like the gods, he knows good and evil ; his eyes are opened ; and his courage has stood the test of disillusionment. He will not again lapse into the backwater of weariness and indecision. His soul is knit to its own purpose. The metal has been tempered in the fire.

MR. JOHN GALSWORTHY

A SHEAF. By John Galsworthy. London : Heinemann.

MR. GALSWORTHY speaks very modestly of this book—the " wild oats of a novelist " he calls it, and adds that he took no wanton pleasure in the sowing. But the book is very much more than a collection of stray papers. It is indeed a tract for the times, none the less timely because much of it was written before the war, and all the more satisfying because it displays exactly the same spirit after that overwhelming disaster as it displayed before it. Mr. Galsworthy had always something of the preacher in his composition. He calls his sermons " pleas " ; but, after all, pleading has always been at least as much the true function of the pulpit as exhortation. And both as a pleader and a moralist Mr. Galsworthy is inspired by that earnest, persuasive influence which can only spring from self-evident and open-hearted sincerity. He is earnest, and he is consistent. The spiritual assaults of the years of war have only served to strengthen in him that deep, humane creed which he urged upon us in the days of universal nonchalance, when we dreamt that we were all at ease in our inns, and that life was going very well in a world of comfortable and comforting convenience. Not many men have faced the facts, both before and after the war, so calmly and dispassionately as Mr. Galsworthy; and few have so much to say that can light up the candelabra in the brain of others. Every page of his book glows with suggestion. His " wild oats " are come to a ripe harvest of sympathy and judgment.

If we were asked to sum up in a phrase the intellectual ideal which Mr. Galsworthy diffuses, we should be inclined to describe it as a sense of proportion. His intellectual standard is the natural standard of the public-school and university man, refined and clarified by the rare capacity to appreciate where our public-school and university product falls short of its own ambition. That standard is indisputably good, so far as it exalts the virtues of self-restraint, of modesty, and of public spirit; it is no less certainly bad in so far as it fosters caste distinctions, splits the nation up into unnecessary and dangerous antagonisms, and represents the unimportant details of conduct and demeanour as the most significant evidences of character and breeding. The world, in which the problem of the proper relations of a turn-over collar and a bow-tie has become a problem by which a man is judged fundamentally and finally, cannot possibly be a world that is ruled by a true and healthy sense of proportion. Yet it was upon trifles like this, a few years back, that social criticism erected its barriers between a man-of-breeding and " a bounder."

But what should be the true standard of difference? What is the καλοκἀγαθός, and what " the bounder?" Mr. Galsworthy's own definition fills the stage to satisfaction. The " gentle man " is he who has " an inborn reverence for due proportion, a natural sense of harmony and rhythm, and a consequent mistrust of extravagance." And his antithesis—the intolerable person—is " just a man without sufficient sense of proportion to know that he is not so important in the scheme of things as he thinks he is." That is an excellent contrast, and it points, perhaps, the only true path to happiness. For the καλοκἀγαθός would see life and all its issues ruled and dominated by the golden law of Nature ; everything physical and spiritual should work out its own salvation upon the lines of its natural and wholesome development. This may seem trite enough as a beginning ; but when the principle gets followed up to its logical conclusions, it throws various illuminating side-lights upon time-worn traditions and customs. For if Nature is to be given her way, it becomes clear that it ought to be as repugnant to a well-balanced mind to see a horse's tail docked to a tar-brush, as to witness the deformity of limb and brain inflicted upon childhood by insanitary life in a fœtid back slum. It follows also that wisdom would regard as the fume of a little mind all that vanity which makes a fuss about the tightness of a skirt or the fulness of a sleeve. " Fashions," says Mr. Galsworthy, " are the guardian angels of vulgarity " : the refined and balanced temperament scorns to change its standards like a milliner's block. It chooses to move along steady, definite lines, to a goal that embodies the triumph of the common welfare.

The attainment of that goal, however, implies

the readjustment of many prevailing concessions to the selfishness of mankind. Take, for example, the ordinary relations between men and animals ; can it be pretended that these relations have been generally dictated by a sense of proportion, or a passion for common justice ? Goldfish in a tiny bowl : a captive coon in a wooden box : a lark in a cage : pigeons in the trap : rabbits on the course : are not these poor suffering creatures the helpless victims of man's obtuse and unbalanced cruelty ? It cannot be right that man should depend for his amusement upon the pain of the weaker part of creation. All unnecessary suffering ought to be eliminated from the wholesome State.

We pass this way but once, but once tread this world, and live in communion with these furred and feathered things, many of them beautiful, in a thousand ways so like ourselves, often friendly if we would let them be, and yet who, one and all, are so simple and helpless in the face of our force and ingenuity. Shall we, as we vanish, say : " I have lived my life as a true lord of creation, taking toll from the captivities and sufferings of every creature that had not my strength and cunning ! " Or shall we pass out with the thought : " I wish I had not given needless pain to any living thing ? "

Needless pain is the scandal of civilisation ; and, where there is a sense of justice as between men and animals, it will soon be found to be established upon a like sense of justice between man and man. But how is such a standard to be maintained ? There are many difficulties to which Mr. Galsworthy hardly gives full weight. At the present time every kind of social pressure pulls the other way. Party politics are the ruin of national harmony, the very bane of a sense of proportion. The essence of party politics is to prevent a man from thinking for himself, to submerge his individuality in a torrent of subordinate and inconsequential interests. The average Englishman rarely pauses to think for himself. He is content to let his newspaper think for him. An extraordinarily false value is attributed in this country to the printed word. Perhaps, if the good-natured citizen could only be persuaded that one-third of everything he reads in a newspaper is dictated by interests of party and place, while another third is designed to capture trade advertisements, his sense of proportion might shake his faith in the noisy authority of Fleet Street. But he goes on his way, good, easy man, butting his head into every obstacle that fate puts in his path ; and so the whole world suddenly finds itself involved in a war which nobody but a few fanatics ever desired, and which all classes of men, in all the nations engulfed, were very soon eagerly desirous of bringing to a speedy end.

And it is when we turn to the problems of the present war that Mr. Galsworthy's own saving sense of proportion appears at last to full advantage. For, surely, if there is any class of men in existence whom the horrors of the prevailing state of Europe might reasonably have driven to distraction, it is that class to which Mr. Galsworthy belongs—a class of men who have persistently preached, in the days of peace, the gospel of a humanity deeper and more spiritual than even our own pacific commercialism had ever conceived. Yet, now that the fire has fallen upon the world, these are found among the very few men who have preserved their intellectual balance and their judgment. You will not find in Mr. Galsworthy's condemnation of the state of war any taint of hysterical excitement, any trace of whimpering or of fear. His sense of proportion is unshaken, simply because he was fore-armed. He has been all his life labouring to defeat cruelty and inhumanity: and now the triumph of the devil's methods gives him his greatest opportunity. Having tasted the poison in small doses, he remains, like Mithridates, impervious to the infection now.

To Mr. Galsworthy Life has always shown a vexed and tearful face; but, as he watches, his eyes seem to fill with the tenderest human sympathy. It is not the irony, but the pity, of it, that obsesses his imagination. Of all living novelists Mr. Galsworthy has, perhaps, the tenderest and most human sense of the prodigality and waste of Life; the sight of suffering moves him indeed to indignation, but it is an indignation that melts almost at once into an eager desire to help and to assuage. He is the humanitarian of modern novelists; the fellow-sufferer whose hand is always extended in the darkness. His sympathy is illimitable; its quickness and intensity almost take away one's breath. There is something subtly feminine about it, and yet it never declines into sentimentality:

> War [he says] is so unutterably tragic, because—without it—Nature, given time, would have attained the same ends in other ways. A war is the spasmodic uprising of old savage instincts against the slow and

gradual humanising of the animal called man. It emanates from restless and so-called virile natures fundamentally intolerant of men's progress towards the understanding of each other—natures that often profess a blasphemous belief in art, a blasphemous alliance with God. It still apparently suffices for a knot of such natures to get together, and play on mass fears and loyalties, to set a continent on fire. And at the end ? Those of us who are able to look back from thirty years hence on this tornado of death will conclude with a dreadful laugh that if it had never come the state of the world would be very much the same.

Out of this intolerable waste, however, it remains for humanity to rebuild the future. " This long and sombre procession of cruelty and suffering " (in Mr. Asquith's moving phrase) must not be allowed to pass and leave the world as it was before. No one can foresee the future ; but it is not too early to begin working for its redemption. Having taken upon us the high duty of crushing evil from without, it would be an unspeakable shame if we allowed ourselves to succumb to evil from within. When once the powers of darkness are defeated, the nation must draw its forces together, must fill its heart with the will to love no less than with the will to power, must choke down all petty internal dissensions, and make of this country of ours, reborn to a nobler peace, a land worthy of the sons who gave their lives for her salvation. " Our future does not lie on the knees of the gods : it lies in our own hands and hearts." Those who survive will be in bondage to the dead, to raise to their glory a memorial of the spirit, more lasting than marble or than brass.

Mr. E. V. LUCAS

Cloud and Silver. By E. V. Lucas. London: Methuen.

IT is quite like old and happier days to find the gentle genius of Mr. E. V. Lucas still fresh and flowering, unchanged by all the changes of this devastating time. I say "unchanged" but, of course, no man, save one of the purely "turnip" type, can really escape the tyranny of his days. In one particularly personal essay Mr. Lucas reminds us that, at the time he wrote it, a couple more "singles" past Old Father Time at cover-point would bring him to the uncoveted half-century; and though it may be true, as the poet says, that

> No bat awaits us in Life's game,
> When we have scored our fifty,

it is at least certain that many other gifts have accrued to us by that time, which separate us inevitably from the dreams and fancies of our youth. Maturity comes, and with it a deeper sense of the pathos of little things, not altogether divorced, perhaps, from an increasing dependence upon creature comforts. The foot "less prompt to meet the morning dew" is no longer content to tramp the open road; and we get suggestions of taxis extravagantly ticking-off the passing moments, and of first-class saloon carriages in close proximity to princesses of the blood. The cosy writing-room, again, has assumed a more elaborate decoration, and a picture from the Royal Academy hangs above the writer's desk. These, it may be, are the tributes of middle-age ; but, after all, they are merely accidentals. Pierce below the surface, and the essential philosopher of the domesticities remains unchanged. The inspired wayfarer, who loved loose and well-worn garments, and called them affectionately " hartogs," is still to be traced in his Parisian restaurant ; the man who took a proprietorial interest in schoolboy hampers still melts at the sight of an Italian waiter, shouting on the top of a cab as he hastens off to join the army ; the same spirit is imperturbably alive to the delight of " dressing-up," even if it be only for the sake of a few seconds' glorification at the camera's mouth. And, even when he follows in the wake of war, it is with the tender sacrifices, the laughter in the trenches, and the good-fellowship of suffering, that he fills his pleasant pages. The smiling philosopher is with us still ; in all the essential qualities of his art he can afford to laugh at Time.

Such personal reflections would seem, perhaps, impertinent, if one were dealing with an artist more impersonal than Mr. Lucas ; but it is the very essence of his work to display his own temperament in all its varied associations. The occasional essay, such as he affects, depends for its very life upon the revelation of temperament; it is a swift record of experiences imbued with the personal impression that holds the secret of its charm. And to touch high-water mark in the art, a writer must be happily free from self-consciousness, or must at least know how to convey the suggestion of absolute ingenuousness and private confidence. The art that secures this effect may be ever so deliberate, but it is imperative that it should not pose. It is the natural reflection of personality; "the adventures of a soul among" trivialities; meditation (so to speak) overheard; and directly the speaker grows conscious of his audience, the charm evaporates.

Few literary arts are more difficult. It is a fact, known to all whose business obliges them to dictate their correspondence, that a letter spoken aloud is seldom so sincere as a letter written by hand. The medium of the recording stenographer distorts the speaker's attitude. No man of honest feeling could possibly dictate a love-letter. And the same risk haunts the occasional, or personal, essay. Most people, when they begin to write about themselves, assume involuntarily the airs of the peacock, and preen their plumage in the sunlight of observation. But Mr. Lucas never makes any such mistake. Almost alone among his contemporaries he can write about himself without the assumption of the egoist. He is self-revealing, but not self-exposing. He never steps over the broad white line which separates personality from conceit. And the reward of his instinctive discretion is that he neither shocks his reader, nor bores him. The charm and the interest of his soliloquies are impregnable.

A friend, more critical than perspicacious, recently told Mr. Lucas (we learn) that his destiny must be to be more amused by people than to amuse them. It was an unfortunate remark, because, as a matter of fact, the very secret of Mr. Lucas's power of amusing his audience lies in his own native amusement in everything that lies around him. And, like all really human amusement, his laughter never strays very far from the paths of seriousness. Take the all-embracing war, for example ; its hold upon the homes of the nation has long been so universal that to write of it in a comic spirit has become hopelessly out of taste and tune. No one outside the nursery takes pleasure any longer in jokes about " Little Willy," or in caricatures of a brutality which has left its mark upon every family in the land. But it is none the less unnecessary to shriek, or to clamour ; melodrama is just as much out of place as farce. To strike the mean is difficult, to be sure ; but Mr. Lucas does so, in the unfailing spirit of human comedy. His pictures of the war are among the most tender and touching that any hand has painted, but the heart of laughter is never far distant from their pathos.

The entire French character is embodied in the story of the Paris restaurant, in the first days of the war, where the voluble French undertaker presses sweet champagne upon les Anglais, thanking them profusely (as though they were themselves the War Office Incarnate) for bringing British troops across the Channel ; while his wife makes a brave show of cordiality in the background, somewhat overshadowed by a hard look about the mouth, " as though she had doubts as to whether the champagne had been quite a necessary expense." Yet all the while, the entire company keeps crying " Vive la France ! " " Vive l'Angleterre ! " to which they add at intervals " A bas les Boches ! " all shaking hands, and bowing, and gesticulating. It is a perfect little masterpiece of genre. And, on a smaller scale, could anything be better than the miniature gallery of studies from the Marne, after the troops have passed, and the villagers are left to their memories and their losses? There is the little boy at Maurupt, who killed a wounded German with the family wood-chopper; the cottager who hid in the forest of the Argonne, with his dog, and after three days of starvation, killed and ate his faithful companion. Yet "he looks just like other men." And again, there is the riverside at Vitry, where all the soldiers fish in the failing evening light, fish, and fish, as though "on that alone hung the issue of the day," catch nothing ever, and still continue fishing. Finally, there is the pale fiancée of the young French officer, spending a few snatched and priceless hours with him in a friendly hotel, whispering of plans for happier days, not with too much confidence, and always with the same aching refrain "Après la guerre!" It is the burden of all the ballads in the world to-day. "Après la guerre!"

But amid the very bitterness of tragedy the sense of humour is always strongest in those who have to endure most. There are moments when the men who are doomed to stay at home can scarcely bear the strain; yet those who have to be doing the Real Thing, find their inspiration in the very necessity of endurance. As their day, so is their strength. And that is why there is laughter in the trenches, and absurdly proud names are given to squalid dug-outs, and the humours of Mr. George Graves and Mr. George

Robey reappear in strange surroundings, and footballs are followed over the parapet, to the cheery cry of " Early doors, sixpence extra ! "

At times, again, the essayist takes us back to those far-off days before the war, when great books were the fruit of great souls, and men had leisure and peace of mind to squander an afternoon in the covered seats at Lord's. A certain calendar has recorded Mr. Lucas's birthday, but by a wayward misprint has substituted a " *d* " for a " *b*." It is on record therefore that the author of this most companionable book " died " in the year 1868, the year, of course, in which he first began to dismay his nurse by that naughty sense of humour, which was never brighter or livelier than in his forty-eighth year ! " And what," he asks, " should I have lost, if I had really died in 1868 ? " There would have been no Thomas Hardy for him to rejoice over, no Stevenson, no Kipling, no W. B. Yeats. He could never have laughed at Fred Leslie or Dan Leno, nor wept with Ellen Terry. He would have died too soon to have seen the triumphs of W. G. Grace, of Stoddart, of Lohmann, and of Trumper. And we, who have enjoyed all these good things, shall not we too be grateful ? The smiling philosopher puts us into the right mood. We shall never see those giants of the greensward again ; they sleep, one and all, beneath the daisies. But we were born in the right hour to see them in their prime. " The gods themselves cannot recall their gifts."

Sursum corda, then. Lift up your hearts. There may be, must be, shadow in the watching home ; but there is laughter in the trenches.

And when the boys come back for the last time (and the heart declines steadfastly to be cheated of that imperishable hope !), when the great day comes, après la guerre, when armistice is at an end, armies of occupation disbanded, and peace signed and sealed, there will be no make-believe then, no " dressing-up " of the emotions, no hiding of the heart's secret vigil. The smiling philosopher will be justified of his good hope, then ! Après la guerre !

THE END

INDEX

Index

Index

Index

Index